The Gift of Values

A Resource for Family Devotions

Rosie Boom

Great Oaks from Little Acorns

The Gift of Values - Volume One.
Copyright © 2006 Rosie Boom

Published by Boom Tree Publishing
549 Kara Rd, R.D. 9 Whangarei 0179, New Zealand
Website: www.rosieboom.com

Rosie Boom contact details:
Email: rosie@rosieboom.com
Rosie's Blog: www.rosieboom.com
Website: www.rosieboom.com

All rights reserved. No part of this book may be reproduced or transmitted in any form or by any means, electronic or mechanical, without prior written permission.

All scripture quotations, unless otherwise indicated, are taken from the HOLY BIBLE, NEW INTERNATIONAL VERSION®. NIV®. Copyright © 1973, 1978, 1984 by International Bible Society. Used by permission of Zondervan. All rights reserved. The Scripture quotations taken from the New American Standard Bible are copyright © 1960, 1962, 1963, 1968, 1971, 1972, 1973, 1975, 1977, 1995 by The Lockman Foundation. Used by permission. www.Lockman.org

Every reasonable effort has been made to trace owners of copyright material in this book, but in some instances this has proved impossible. The publisher will be glad to receive information leading to more complete acknowledgements in subsequent printings of the book, and in the meantime extends apologies for any omissions.

Cover Design by Stephen Cooling
Printed and bound by Lightning Source

National Library of Australia Cataloguing-in-Publication

Boom, Rosie, 1956-
 The Gift of Values. Vol 1, A Devotional Resource for Families.

 1st ed.
 ISBN 9781921161056 (hbk.).

 1. Family 2. Moral education. 3. Christian Life. 4. Values clarification. I. Title

 248.845

 2nd ed.
 ISBN 978-0-9951123-4-6

This book is for you, Chris. You were worth the wait!
And for my children ~
Josiah, Kate, Eliza, Emily, Samuel and Jacob ~
my cup overflows.
God has been good to me.

"The Gift of Values has sparked my joy for teaching character-building devotions to my children, and has injected wonder and enthusiasm into the experience. Here is a tool that will help make these precious times even more memorable, fun-filled, and a real learning adventure. I appreciate the honest, real-life touches throughout the book. I'm certain that with the aid of this book, God will draw many little hearts even closer to Him."

Chris Bovill
Mother of five and Co-ordinator of HEART
(Home Educators Annual Retreat), Morrinsville, New Zealand

"This book is just fantastic – it is everything that I longed for as a young parent. Rosie Boom has produced an outstanding resource for parents. As a young mother, I spent many hours scouring bookshops and parenting magazines for help in creating family times with our children. I searched for material which taught Christian truths, was inspirational, and which captured the hearts of our youngsters. This book is what I was looking for. Put together with so much love and care, it will be treasured by parents everywhere. Rosie's passion for educating children, her mother's heart and her concern for her children's character all shine through.

But most of all there is something for everyone. The background reading for parents, the stories, mottos, proverbs and sayings for children and the real-life examples from Rosie herself, all add up to a very special publication. I could not recommend this book more highly to all parents, whether Christian or not, who are committed to leaving their children a legacy of character and insight."

Mary Grant
Co-founder of Parents Inc., Editor of Parenting magazine, Auckland, New Zealand

"A wonderful resource that will be a gem of a book to many parents. Filled with creative ideas, anecdotes and inspiration, this book will be returned to again and again by both parents and children. I heartily recommend it to you."

Don Barry
Senior Leader Gateway Christian Centre, Hamilton, New Zealand

"What mother wouldn't want this book? What mother doesn't need this book?"

Penelope Foote
Mother of five, Whangarei, New Zealand

"This book is a valuable resource for parents in their important but often difficult task of bringing up a family and instilling good values into young lives. It is full of practical suggestions and creative ideas, drawing on the wisdom of the past, the author's experience of the present and the teaching of Scripture."

Dr John Sturt
Counsellor, Auckland

"What an awesome book. It is practical, honest, and contains such powerful keys to raising children in the ways of the Master. Rosie's heart is poured out through this book, and the love and devotion she has for Jesus is contagious.
We highly recommend this excellent book for every one to read."

Ian and Jane McCormack
Evangelists, parents of three, Tauranga, New Zealand

S. D. G.

The Gift of Values ~ Tabs

Value One HONESTY .... 9

Value Two A POSITIVE ATTITUDE .... 31

Value Three COURAGE .... 53

Value Four DILIGENCE .... 77

Value Five PERSEVERANCE .... 95

Value Six OBEDIENCE .... 113

The Shema

Hear O Israel; the Lord our God, the Lord is one. Love the Lord your God with all your heart and with all your soul and with all your strength. These commandments that I give you today are to be upon your hearts. Impress them on your children. Talk about them when you sit at home and when you walk along the road, when you lie down and when you get up. Tie them as symbols on your hands and bind them on your foreheads. Write them on the doorframes of your house and on your gates.

Deuteronomy 6:4-9

The Gift of Values

Contents

Preface 1

How to use this book 3

Value One HONESTY 9
    George and the Cherry Tree 11
    Blackball Stains 18
    The Emperor and the Seed 24

Value Two A POSITIVE ATTITUDE 31
    Don't Cry Over Spilt Milk 33
    The Unfortunate Man 38
    Who Am I? 46

Value Three COURAGE 53
    Riot in the Prison 55
    Orange in a Sea of Grey 60
    A Foolish Dare 65
    Flynn of Thrim 70

Value Four DILIGENCE 77
   The Elephant's Trunk 79
   A Pocket of Beans 84
   The Ants and the Grasshopper 88

Value Five PERSEVERANCE 95
   "I Can Plod" 96
   "You're Just Not Suited!" 103
   Wheelbarrow Jack 107

Value Six OBEDIENCE 113
   "Who, me?!" 119
   The Widow's Birthday 125
   The Knights of the Silver Shield 130

How to do a Bible study 138

Epilogue 140

Acknowledgements 141

More from the Boom family album 143

About the Author 148

Preface

I couldn't wait to write this book. For many years I've dreamed about having time to write down some of the things that have worked in our family, and share them with others.

With six busy, noisy children, free time is not something I have a lot of. I teach the children at home, and although it is one of the greatest joys of my life, home-schooling is both demanding and time consuming. However, Jacob, my youngest will be six next week, and I have just finished applying for my last home-schooling exemption today! That makes me very aware that nothing lasts forever. Josiah, our firstborn, will be seventeen this year. I am very conscious of how little time we have left with him in our home, and I'm so grateful I have been able to home-school him all these years. Yes, I still feel sad when I think about him leaving home, but I'm not consumed with regrets over all the things I wish I'd done with him, and the time I should have spent with him. That is the greatest gift home-schooling has given me - TIME. Time with my children, time to disciple them in the ways of the Lord, time to enjoy them.

For the past twelve years, the children and I have cuddled up on the sofa each morning and enjoyed devotions together. This is the heart of our home-schooling. We take as long as we like and don't skimp on this all important part of our day. Over the years we've studied the Bible, read hundreds of stories, worked our way through many inspiring devotionals, and devoured countless biographies. Every six months, I have used a portion of my home-schooling money to purchase devotional books, and have amassed quite a collection. While being very aware of all the wonderful books available on this topic, I have had a persistent urge to write yet another one, relating our own journey and the things that have 'worked' in our family.

My aim in writing this book is to give you, the parent, a resource you can use in your own family devotions - something that is simple and usable. I don't want you to have to wade through pages of writing just to glean a few things that you can integrate into your own family experience. I have laid it out in such a way that you can pick it up and follow it through step by step. Alternatively, you can use one small portion at a time. I have deliberately *not* made this an exhaustive study of each topic, despite the very real temptation! I have tried to keep it fairly streamlined and un-daunting.

For those of you who have children in school, the thought of having family devotions may seem like the straw that would break the camel's back. I'm aware of the hectic rush it can be in the morning to get your children off to school on time. I hope this book will be so easy to read and use, that you will feel inspired to snatch even just a few moments of your busy day and enjoy some special time with your child. Remember, every moment counts. We can feel discouraged if we don't achieve all our goals, but rather, we should be celebrating every small step along the way. If you feel daunted at the idea of family devotions, start small. But try to make it a habit. Remember, great oaks grow from little acorns!

For those of you who have struggled with family devotions, and found them more a curse than a blessing, my hope is that this book will make you think, "I can do this!"

And for those of you who have yet to embark on the wonderful journey of family devotions, my prayer is that this book will be just what you need to get you started.

This is my gift to you.

How to use this book

The fact that you are reading this book indicates you have a desire to instil in your children a love for God, a thirst for truth, and a solid foundation of true values.

We all long to see our children develop a strong character - a character which will help them navigate their way through this ungodly world, not just by the skin of their teeth, but as shining examples to others.

We have the awesome responsibility of planting the seed of God's word in the hearts of our children. Within the seed of strong, clear moral values lies the fruit of joy and personal fulfillment. Our children will lead happier and more fulfilling lives if they have a strong foundation of Christian values.

It is never too early (or too late) to start. Some of you reading this may be thinking, "How can I possibly teach my children the values of honesty and forgiveness when my own life has been such a mess? Aren't I being hypocritical trying to teach my children something that I am still struggling with myself?"

Absolutely not! You can teach your children not only from the things you've done well, but also from the things that you wished you'd done differently. Richard Eyre writes in his book *Teaching Your Children Values*, "We all want to teach better than we ourselves have learned. We all want our children to surpass us." Amen to that!

I have written this book with my own family in mind, aware that many of you also have families with a fairly big spread of ages. Ideally, we want to make devotions a time which all the children enjoy. This can be a challenge, but I believe it can be done. I have included stories that will appeal to the younger ones, and that the older ones can listen in to as well. Always be thinking of age-appropriate questions that you can ask each of the children. I have included thought provoking quotes for the older children. In our own family, I have generally stayed with one value for at least a fortnight. That way, the children become aware of it in their own lives, and begin to look for examples of it in the books they read and in everyday life. My suggestion would be to read the first story, and ask questions on the first day. Over the next few days, you could look at the Bible references and discuss some of the quotes. Enjoy plenty of discussion times. Choose further readings from the suggested reading list. There are plenty of ideas for further developments if you so choose. I hope it's all here for you - a small bite if that's all you have time for, or a three course meal if you're hungry!

Each chapter includes the following…

Stories

The words 'Once upon a time' never fail to thrill me. A story can move you; challenge you; open your eyes. There is nothing like a good story to get a truth across. Jesus knew that. He was a master storyteller.

In each chapter I have included stories that you can share with your children, and suggestions for further reading as well. But don't forget - your own life is a book full of wonderful stories you can share with your children. You may never become a children's writer, but you can learn to tell your own stories. Your children will love to hear you share about your own life. As you read a new chapter, ask God to remind you of any thing in your life that will help apply the truth. It may be just a small incident that happened when you were a child, but as you share it, it will have real impact. And once you start looking for these 'stories', you'll find them everywhere.

Encourage your children to tell their own stories as well. You'll be amazed how even the youngest can tell something so pertinent to the value that you're talking about. It only takes one of them to say, "I remember when…" and the others will be bursting to have their say.

Think about it

Jesus asked a lot of questions. He wanted people to search out truth for themselves. Get into the habit of asking lots of questions in your devotional time. Get your children thinking. Once you develop the habit, you'll find it becomes very easy to think of thought provoking questions, even while you're reading a story. I have included some prompts to get the ball rolling.

Something to do

Over the years, I've tried to think of practical, creative ways I can illustrate a truth that we've been learning about in our devotional times. I'll share some of these in each chapter, and they'll probably be the only prompt you need to think of plenty of your own. Van Dyke once said, *"Opportunities swarm around us, thicker than gnats at sundown. Every day we walk through a swarm of them."* Creative ideas are like that. Once you train your eyes to see them, they come thick and fast. But you have to be looking for them.

And if you feel you haven't got a creative bone in your body - don't worry! Creative ideas are given by God to be shared. Borrow the ideas of others and make them your own. There are plenty enough ideas to go around!

So said...

A few carefully crafted words can hold so much truth and meaning. They offer great starting points for lively discussion. The quotes I list in each chapter are just the tip of a huge iceberg. Go hunting yourself and pin them up in different places around your house. A notice board in the 'little room' is a great place for displaying your finds!

Words to live by

There are countless scriptures that apply to each topic, but I have listed just a few as a starting point. If you have older children, encourage them to use these as a springboard for their own Bible studies. I've written a short explanation at the back of the book of how to do a simple, but very effective Bible study. This is the way I used to study the Bible when I first became a Christian as a sixteen year old. Simple, yes, but it has been a huge source of blessing to me. I still have all the studies I did as a teenager - over thirty years ago! Go through it with your older children and encourage them to begin. Once they do, they'll never stop.

Boom clip

In this book, I have shared with you many personal experiences and anecdotes that have happened in the Boom household. We are a very normal family, and have had plenty of 'learning' moments - squabbles, fights, disagreements, dramas etc. But we have also had a rich, endless supply of joy and laughter!

Dig deeper

As much as possible, get your children to do some research on the topic. A simple idea is to get one of them to look up the particular word in the dictionary. Just discussing some of the listed meanings will offer a goldmine.

Another thing the older children can do is search the internet for more quotes. A caution here. The internet is a mine field, and quotes can be a storehouse for offensive material. I always type in 'Inspirational quotes on…' in the search engine, and have not read an offensive one yet. However, the one time I left the word 'inspirational' out, I was bombarded with some really dubious quotes.

There are many different ways you can develop the basic ideas in this book. There are countless movies that illustrate the different truths and an endless supply of books and biographies you can enjoy. At the end of each chapter I have listed books or videos which we as a family have enjoyed, that have helped reinforce the appropriate truth.

A great resource we have used is Focus on the Family's entertainment review site, *www.pluggedinonline.com*. Here you can get a detailed review of a big selection of movies and videos from a Christian perspective. It lists each occurrence of bad language, violence or sexual content, and gives a good overview of the movie's plot. If you want to enjoy a relaxed movie evening with the family, without feeling on edge and wondering what's going to come on the screen next, check it out on this site first.

☙

One last word...

Recently I read a great pithy saying: "Think it, ink it." In other words, write things down! We forget so easily - even things we're sure we'll never forget! Get into the habit of writing things down. Aside from helping you to remember, it serves to solidify and clarify what you've learnt. It also ensures that later you can go back and "Do it, review it!" (As the second half of the saying goes.)

I hope that as you work through this book, you will encourage your children to do lots of 'inking!' When each of my children turned four years old, I gave them a big, blank book. It is *the* place to write down scriptures that they're memorizing, great quotes, poems - anything that is inspiring and worthy of remembering. The children do art work in there as well. It was one of the best things I ever did. I encourage you to do the same. Make sure you get a well bound book with good quality art paper - you want it to last. This will be a book each child treasures as they grow older. They aren't expensive, but even if they were, they'd be worth every cent!

As your children learn about the values covered by this book and try to put them into practice, watch them carefully - not so much for what they do wrong, but for what they do right. Look for every opportunity you can to praise them. Reinforce and acknowledge their attempts to be kind or honest. For example, Samuel has just this minute run in to tell me that Jacob has fallen off the tramp and hurt himself. I praise him for being kind and caring, and his face glows.

Praise your children for every little step they take in the right direction, and give plenty of encouragement along the way. The Duke of Wellington was asked near the end of his life what one thing he would change if he could live his life over again. "I would give more praise," he replied.

May God bless you as you embark on this wonderful journey.

Value One

HONESTY

Teaching honesty to children can be a real challenge. Inherent in the fallen nature of each one of us is the tendency to lie to save our necks, or to gain something we really want.

Just today I had a wonderful example of honesty. As I waited in line at a supermarket check out, the lady in front of me paid for her groceries, and then handed the operator a dollar coin. "I was under charged a dollar yesterday," she told the operator. The surprised young check out operator hesitated for a moment, unsure of quite what she should do. Then she took the coin with a thank you, and dropped it in the charity box by the till.

Just a small vignette of a value we don't see so much these days - the surprise and confusion on the check out operator's face attested to that. But I couldn't help thinking what a powerful example it was. The fact that the girl dropped the money into the charity box had a real impact on me. I realized that honesty is always a gift. Every time we choose honesty over cheating or lying, we are offering a gift to someone - the gift of honesty. Conversely, every time we choose to lie, we are robbing someone - perhaps of their trust, or faith or hope.

I don't think any of us will be lacking examples to share with our children of how we've been backed into a corner and have lied our way out. But we also need to try and remember as many examples we can of how we have chosen to be honest even when it hurt us.

The Gift of Values

Another point: make sure your children realize that this is not just a 'children's' issue and challenge. All our lives we will be faced with choosing honesty. Adults are just as adept at lying as children - perhaps even more so. But if your children learn to choose honesty even under pressure while they are young, it will be a whole lot easier for them to do so when they're older.

George and the Cherry Tree
Adapted from J. Berg Esenwein and Marietta Stockard

George lived as a small lad on a farm in Virginia. His father taught him how to ride, and how to care for the cattle and fields. The Washingtons had a fine orchard, full of plum trees, apple trees, peach and pear trees. One day, a cherry tree was sent as a gift to George's father from overseas. He carefully planted it in his orchard and instructed everyone to be very careful that it didn't get broken or damaged in any way.

The cherry tree thrived, and come spring, it was covered in white blossoms. Mr Washington was delighted! Soon they would enjoy fresh cherries.

At this time, George received a gift of a shiny new hatchet. It was very sharp, and he had a great time chopping up wood and sticks, and even hacking into the wooden fence rails. It was fantastic! At last he came to the edge of the orchard, and thinking only of how well his hatchet was cutting, he chopped into the little cherry tree. The bark was soft, and the tree fell to the ground.

George was horrified. What would his father say when he saw it?

That evening, his father walked through the orchard and saw the tree. He stared in amazement. Who would have dared to do such a thing? Just then George passed by.

"George," said his father in an angry voice, "do you know who killed my cherry tree?"

George's mouth felt dry. He swallowed a few times then said, "I cannot tell a lie, Father. I did it with my hatchet."

Mr. Washington looked at his son's white face. "Go into the house, son," he said sternly.

George waited in the library. He felt ashamed. *If only he had thought!* He looked up as his father entered the room.

The Gift of Values

"Come here, my boy."

George went to his father, who looked at him for a long moment. "Tell me, son, why did you cut the tree?"

"I was playing with my new hatchet and I didn't think...," stuttered George.

"And now the tree will die. We shall never enjoy its cherries. But worse than that, you have failed to take care of the tree when I asked you to do so." His father's face was grave.

George bent his head in shame. His cheeks flushed bright red.

"I'm sorry, Father," he said.

Then Mr. Washington laid his hand on his son's shoulder. "Look at me," he said. "I am very sorry to have lost my tree, but I am glad that you were brave enough to tell me the truth. I would rather have you truthful and brave than have a whole orchard full of cherry trees. Never forget that, son."

George Washington never did forget. He tried to live an honest life to the end of his days.

Think about it

- ❖ Have you ever been so carried away with something you were doing, that you did something foolish?
- ❖ Discuss the old adage, "Stop and think!"
- ❖ What do you think would have happened if George had denied chopping the cherry tree down?
- ❖ How do you think he felt when his father responded the way he did?
- ❖ Why did his father call him honest *and* brave?
- ❖ Every time we come to God and ask Him to forgive us for something we have done wrong, we are doing what George did. We are taking responsibility for our actions and seeking to put things right. Discuss

the concept with your older children that honesty often involves repentance, and the words, "I'm sorry. Forgive me."

Something to do

- Design your own honesty reward. Present it each evening at dinner to whichever child has been honest even when it's been hard to be so. A word to mums and dads! Make sure you reward honesty. Even if your best jug lies shattered on the floor, praise your child if they have had the courage to come and tell you about it straight away. They can still bear certain consequences for their actions, but don't punish them.

- Make a cherry pie for dessert, and as you enjoy eating it, see if the children can retell the story of George Washington and the cherry tree.

Cherry Pie

What You Need

25 cm baking dish
40gms butter
500gms cherries (fresh or frozen and defrosted, stones removed)
5 tablespoons castor sugar
3 large eggs
3 tablespoons plain flour
Pinch of salt
450mls milk

Method

1. Set oven to 200 C
2. Lightly butter baking dish. Place cherries in dish.
3. Beat eggs, flour, salt, and 3 tablespoons of the sugar in a bowl until smooth.
4. Heat the milk until almost boiling. It will start to steam gently when it's ready. Pour milk over egg mixture and beat until smooth.

5. Pour egg and milk mixture over the cherries. Cut remaining butter into slivers and scatter them over pudding.
6. Place baking dish in a roasting tin. Carefully pour warm water into roasting dish to come halfway up the baking dish sides. Place dish in oven for 35 – 40 minutes until the batter is set like a custard and lightly golden. Sprinkle with remaining sugar and serve warm.

So said...

- "Our lives improve only when we take chances - and the first and most difficult risk we can take is to be honest with ourselves." *Walter Anderson*

- "Prefer a loss to a dishonest gain; the one brings pain at the moment, the other for all time." *Chilton*

- "Honesty is the first chapter of the book of wisdom." *Thomas Jefferson*

- "No legacy is so rich as honesty." *William Shakespeare*

- "Son, always tell the truth. Then you'll never have to remember what you said the last time." *Sam Rayburn*

- "A lie has speed, but truth has endurance." *Edgar J. Mohn*

- "I hope I shall always possess firmness and virtue enough to maintain what I consider the most enviable of all titles, the character of an honest man." *George Washington*

- "To be persuasive we must be believable; to be believable we must be credible; to be credible we must be truthful." *Edward R. Murrow*

- "Honesty is vital for success in business as in life." *M. K. Soni*

- "The truth is more important than the facts." *Frank Lloyd Wright*

- "Clear conscience never fears midnight knocking." *Chinese proverb*

❖ "There is no pillow so soft as a clear conscience." *French proverb*

Boom clip

I had only just prayed with my daughter a few minutes earlier and tucked her in bed. But there was the noise again. I put my book down and listened. Yes, there was no doubt about it. Ellie was crying. I went back to her room and sat on her bed. "What's the matter, honey?" I asked.

She sat up in bed and threw her arms around me. "Oh, Mummy," she sobbed. "I've been keeping a bad secret."

"Well, would you like to tell me about it?" I asked gently.

She nodded miserably. "Last week Milly took a little soft toy from a shop and told me not to tell you. We've been playing with it together. We were going to take it back and pay for it next time we were in that shop. Honest, Mum!"

I looked at my young daughter. "But I don't understand," I said. "Why have you chosen to tell me about it now?"

"Because of the movie, Mum! I want to be able to enjoy the movie!"

Ah. Suddenly I understood. Ellie had been so excited about going to see a movie with her friend the next day. But as she lay in bed, she knew her conscience wasn't clean. She wanted to put things right so there'd be no reason for her not to fully enjoy her special day. What a wonderful gift the conscience is!

We prayed together and then we talked about what she would have to do to put things right. Never mind that she had to go with Milly and apologize to the shop keeper. Never mind that she had to help pay for the toy. That night she went to sleep with a smile on her face and a clean conscience. Tomorrow would be a good day.

Words to live by

- "So I strive always to keep my conscience clear before God and man." *Acts 24:16 NIV*

- "Our conscience testifies that we have conducted ourselves in the world, and especially in our relations with you, in the holiness and sincerity that are from God." *2 Corinthians 1:12 NIV*

- "The goal of this command is love, which comes from a pure heart and a good conscience and a sincere faith." *1 Timothy 1:5 NIV*

- "Timothy, my son, I give you this instruction in keeping with the prophecies once made about you, so that by following them you may fight the good fight, holding onto faith and a good conscience. Some have rejected these and so have shipwrecked their faith." *1 Timothy 1:18, 19 NIV*

Dig deeper

- Read *Pinocchio* or watch the video.

- Watch *Les Miserables* with the older children. Jean Valjean is faced with a choice. He can either let a simple minded fellow be convicted instead of himself, or else he can reveal that he is in fact the one the authorities are looking for. It is a wonderful example of choosing honesty even at great personal cost.

- Read *The Boy who Cried Wolf* with the younger children and discuss.

- Watch the video *Anne of Green Gables* or read the book. It has plenty of examples of honesty. My favourite is the episode of the dead mouse in the milk.

- Watch the video *Little Men*. It deals with issues of honesty and integrity. Our whole family has enjoyed it.

- Read about Abraham Lincoln. He once walked three miles to give a lady six and a quarter cents when he realized he had over charged her. At one time in his life he owned a grocery store. The store failed, but Abraham Lincoln voluntarily paid off all his debts, an act for which he earned the name 'Honest Abe'. His mother told him, "Being poor is nothing to be ashamed about. As long as you are honest, and you respect other people, they will respect you no matter how poor you are!"

- Listen to Billy Joel's song *Honesty* and discuss.

Blackball Stains

Altus licked his lips and hastily wiped his mouth with his sleeve as he walked toward the front door. He'd be in big trouble if his mother found out what he'd done.

"Hi, Mum! Got the bread," he called out. He put the loaf on the table and turned to hurry outside before she saw him.

"Thank you, Altus," said Mum, as she came through the door. She stopped wiping her hands on her apron, and looked hard at her son's face. Black sticky stains darkened his lips and smudged onto one cheek.

Under his mother's gaze, Altus felt his stomach squirming inside.

"When's lunch?" he asked, hoping to ease the panic he felt. When he spoke, his tongue was blackish-purple, and even his teeth were discoloured.

His mother looked at him a moment longer, and then asked quietly, "Can I have the change please, son?"

Altus's eyes flicked toward the door and he swallowed nervously. "Louis didn't give me any." Even as he said it, Altus felt shame wash over him. Louis, the Portuguese shop keeper, had always been kind to him.

"But Altus," said Mum ever so quietly, "half a loaf of bread only costs three cents. I gave you five."

Altus felt trapped. He looked down at the floor and said in a surly voice, "Well, he didn't give me any change."

Mum sighed and looked at her son. It was dusty and hot in South Africa at this time of the year, and grime covered his bare feet. His face was streaked with dirt, and the telltale sign of blackballs.

"Well, darling, you'd better run back to the shop and ask him for the two cents change."

Now what? thought Altus as he slowly trudged back to the shop.

Louis looked up and smiled as Altus entered the shop.

Honesty

Altus fixed his eyes on a large jar of gob stoppers before he spoke. "Mum says you need to give me two cents change."

Louis looked straight at him. "No," he said slowly. "The bread cost three cents and you spent the rest of it on blackballs."

Altus didn't know what else to say. He turned and left without even so much as a glance at the shopkeeper. The walk home took forever. His head hurt and his stomach felt all churned up, almost like he was going to be sick. All the *if-onlys* tumbled around inside his head until it throbbed. If only he hadn't bought those stupid blackballs. If only he'd just taken the money home to Mum like he knew he should have. How could he get out of this mess now? What could he tell her so she wouldn't guess the truth?

Altus kicked at a stone. "Ouch!" He sat down on the roadside and squeezed his stubbed toe hard to try to stop the stinging. Hot, angry tears filled his eyes. What were a few measly sweets anyway? He wiped away the tears. He knew the answer. They didn't have a lot of money, and two cents was nearly enough for another half loaf of bread. Shame and anger tumbled around inside him. *Maybe I should just tell her the truth,* he thought as he got to his feet.

Ten minutes later he limped into the kitchen and sat down at the table.

"Did you get the change?" asked Mum.

Altus stared at his bleeding toe for a long moment and then whispered, "Louis said there wasn't any change." He winced as he caught the look on his mother's face.

"Are you sure?" asked Mum.

Altus nodded miserably.

"Right," said Mum. "Hop in the car. We'll go there together and sort it out."

Altus felt a bitter taste in his mouth as he looked out the car window. *Why didn't I just own up right at the start? Why did I bring Louis into it?* He glanced across at his mum. Her lips looked tight and he could see a

The Gift of Values

muscle twitching in her cheek. He quickly looked away. *Oh boy, she'll be really mad when she finds out I've been lying to her.*

Mum walked into Louis' shop in a no-nonsense way. Altus knew that walk. His own feet dragged, and felt as if they were made of lead.

"Hello, Louis," said Mum cheerfully. "There seems to be a mix-up. Altus didn't bring any change home. Has the price of bread gone up?"

Louis and Mum both turned and looked at Altus. He squirmed and looked down at the floor. Why were they looking at his mouth that way? Unconsciously he wiped his mouth on his sleeve.

They seemed to be waiting for him to say something.

Finally Louis spoke. "No, ma'am. Your boy spent the other two cents on some blackballs."

I'm done for, thought Altus. But then a strange feeling of relief flooded through him. It was over. He could handle the punishment that was coming to him. At least he wouldn't have the awful feeling of being trapped in a spider's web.

"Thank you, Louis. I'm sorry to have been a bother," said Mum. Altus felt her hand firmly on his shoulder, guiding him out to the car.

"As soon as we get home, Altus," said Mum, "I want you to go and have a good look in the mirror. Then we'll talk about the lies you've just told. When we hide sin in our hearts, it's as obvious to God as the black stains on your face."

Altus nodded.

"Tomorrow you can pay another visit to Louis to apologize," said Mum. She smiled at her son's sad, black-stained face. "I wonder whether he would appreciate someone sweeping his floors for the next week or so?"

Think about it

- ❖ What are some of the consequences of honesty? (People trust you; you know the blessings of peace, joy, self respect, confidence.)

Honesty

- What about the consequences of lying? (You earn the mistrust of people; you get caught out eventually; lack of self respect; lying destroys relationships; you begin to mistrust others.)

- Can you think of any short term benefits or solutions of dishonesty? E.g: a medical student cheats in his tests. He may get an A, but deep down inside he knows he didn't deserve it. How does that make him feel? Will he feel confident as a doctor?

- What would you do if you found a gold necklace on the road?

- Is honesty easy? (No. Often you are feeling ashamed of what you've done and it's very tempting to hide it. One of the easiest lies to slip off our tongues is, "It wasn't me!")

- Why is it so hard to tell the truth? (You may worry about people being mad at you. Or you may fear the cost of putting things right. Perhaps it's very embarrassing to own up to something.)

- How is it possible to 'bend' the truth? (Exaggeration, omitting certain facts, keeping silent when we should speak up; a witness who refuses to testify.)

Boom clip

My children love to hear the story of when I went to stay the night at my school friend's place. When it came time to get ready for bed I realized I had forgotten my toothbrush. I felt awfully guilty doing it, but I still did it - I used my friend's toothbrush. Seconds later she came in and picked up her toothbrush. It was still wet. "Did you use my toothbrush?" she asked, looking horrified. I was so embarrassed. "Of course not!" I replied with a sick feeling in my stomach. If only that had been the end of it.

The Gift of Values

She charged out of the bathroom and demanded to know who among her family had been so gross as to use her toothbrush. Of course they all denied it and they all had very good alibis. It was obvious to everyone that I was the culprit. I wanted to crawl under the carpet. At least if I'd owned up to it straight away, the whole family wouldn't have known about it. Ah well. We live and learn.

Something to do

- ❖ Play a detective game. Call each child out into the kitchen one by one and give them a sweet to eat. But give one of them a piece of some different sweet that will discolour their tongue. Then let them all work out who had the different sweet. It will be quite simple. Remind them that our sins are just as obvious to God - there is nothing hidden in His sight.

- ❖ Play an honesty game. Write a short scenario with two possible courses of action - honesty and dishonesty. Have the children think about the consequences of each option.

For example: *Scenario One:* Suzie buys a new necklace at a shop and the shopkeeper gives her $10 too much change. She decides not to say anything. After all, the shopkeeper should be more careful. She goes next door and buys a DVD that she's always wanted that happens to be on special.

Consequence: Suzie knows deep down she should have pointed out the mistake. And every time she watches the DVD she feels guilty, and can't enjoy it.

Scenario Two: Suzie sees that the shopkeeper has made a mistake with her change and hands the $10 back to him. He thanks her. She goes next door and sees the DVD on special and realizes she could have bought it if she'd kept the money.

Consequence: Suzie feels good inside because she was honest. She knows she'll be able to buy other things at the jewellery store without feeling guilty when she enters the shop. When she saves enough money to buy the DVD she remembers every time she watches it that she was honest.

Words to live by

- "Come my children, listen to me and I will teach you the fear of the Lord. Who is the man who desires life, and loves length of days that he may see good? Keep your tongue from evil and your lips from speaking lies." *Psalm 34:11-13*

- Gehazi first lies to Naaman, and then to Elisha. Discuss the consequences of his deceit. *2 Kings 5:15-27*

So said...

- "We cannot forever hide the truth about ourselves, from ourselves." *John McCain*

- "If you tell the truth you don't have to remember anything." *Mark Twain*

- "The next time you make a mistake, go directly to the one you wronged, admit it, and watch what God will do. Pick up your courage; walk past your fears; speak the truth. It's the man's road to freedom." *Bob Schultz*

Dig deeper

- Read *Max and the Big Fat Lie* by Michael P. Waite. It's a fun poem about a boy who really wants to watch a video that he knows his mother wouldn't approve of. There is a knock at his bedroom door and in comes Sir Fib with a great suggestion.

The Gift of Values

The Emperor and the Seed
Adapted from a Chinese Folk Tale

Many years ago in the Far East, an Emperor proclaimed that he would soon choose a bride for his son. She must be wise and honest, as well as beautiful. All eligible maidens were invited to come to the palace on the first day of the full moon. For days after the announcement, the noble women in the land preened and fussed before their mirrors, until their hair shone as black as the coat of the Emperor's stallion.

On the due date, the courtyard of the palace was filled with hopeful women. Among them was a young girl named Ling. She was the only daughter of a poor widow. *I am like a weed amongst the roses,* she thought to herself as she looked at all the women in their magnificent clothes and jewels. She glanced down at her own shabby clothes, and brushed at the garden dirt that clung to her dress.

A hush came over the crowd as the Emperor's messenger opened a scroll and began to read. "The great Emperor has decreed that a wife shall be chosen from among you for his son. Each of you shall be given a special seed. You must plant this seed and water it and care for it. When the moon is full in the skies again you must return to the palace with your seed. The Emperor shall judge your plant and then make his choice of a bride for his son."

A hum filled the courtyard. Could it possibly be? Was the Emperor no longer concerned about noble blood and their kingdom's traditions and customs?

Ling trembled as the tiny black seed was placed in her hand. She quickly closed her hand, lest the Emperor's servant should see the calluses that lay across her palm.

"You must take the greatest care of this seed," her mother told Ling that evening. "Take some of the richest soil from our garden, and plant it in our best pot. Perhaps the sun of good fortune will shine again on our family."

That night Ling went to sleep and dreamed of the prince.

The days passed slowly. Ling ran home each evening after her work in the fields was done, and checked her seed. But each night it was the same. No tender shoot appeared from the black soil. She set the pot in the gentle morning sun, and placed it in the shade when the sun burned hot. Ling sang to her seed by the light of the half empty moon. But still it refused to grow.

"What shall I do?" she cried as she lay with her head in her mother's lap. "Today in the market place all the women spoke of the wonderful plants that are growing from their seeds. And I have nothing to show the Emperor! Nothing!"

"Rest, my Ling," her mother answered. "You are doing all that you can."

The next night the moon was nowhere to be seen in the skies. "Fourteen more days until I must return to the palace," Ling told her mother as she lit the evening fire. "Surely tomorrow is the day my seed will grow."

She woke early the next morning and ran to the window ledge to see if the seed had sprouted. It had not.

Days passed. When the moon was half full again, Ling said with a hopeful voice, "Only seven more days before I must return to the palace. Surely tomorrow will be the day! For I have sung to my seed and watered it and cared for it. It must yield its harvest soon."

The next evening after she hurried home with water from the well, Ling placed the heavy jug on the floor and ran to her room. But the clay pot sat empty and barren.

"Mother," she cried. "This is worse than walking into a web of spiders. The entire kingdom will laugh at me."

"Do your best, daughter," replied her mother. "That is all you can do."

The Gift of Values

The next few days passed slowly for Ling. As she beat the clothes in the river and hung them on the rocks to dry, she dreamed of the prince. And as she milked the goat, and stirred the rice, she could think of nothing else.

Finally the last day dawned. Ling went about her chores with a heavy heart, for still her seed refused to yield its treasures. That night as she sat with her mother on the dirt floor of their small hut, Ling wept.

The silver light of the full moon shone on her tears.

"Ah, my daughter," soothed her mother, "be at rest. Even if the whole kingdom should laugh, I shall be proud of you tomorrow. You have done your best. Perhaps you were not meant to be the prince's bride."

The next morning Ling awoke early and set off for the palace. She did not hurry. By the time she reached the great gates, the courtyard was crowded with women. Ling gasped. The air was thick with the sweetest perfume. Beautiful lilies and roses and exotic flowers shone within each expensive pot. Ling glanced down at her clay pot full of barren soil, and her stomach twisted. Perhaps the Emperor would be angry?

At that moment a silver trumpet blew and the Emperor entered the courtyard. Everyone bowed low.

"Today, I shall choose a bride for the Prince," said the Emperor. "Let the judging begin."

One by one the women filed forward and showed their plants. Ling's heart pounded in her chest. She wanted to run home to her mother and forget her foolish dreams. She edged to the back of the line. Just then the Emperor caught sight of Ling and her empty pot. "Come!" he ordered.

The crowd parted as Ling slowly walked forward. Ripples of laughter grew into a loud swell as Ling made her way towards the Emperor. "Silence!" he cried.

"What is your name?"

Ling bowed low. "My name is Ling, Your Highness."

The Emperor rose from his seat and raised a hand to the crowd. "One month ago," he said in a loud voice, "I gave each of you a seed. Many of you have returned with strong, healthy plants. But they are not from the seeds I gave you."

A hush filled the room as the Emperor's sharp eyes scanned the courtyard. Then a small smile crept to his eyes, and he laughed out loud.

"I had my seeds boiled in oil," he said, "then dried in the sun. There was no life in them. My seeds could never grow."

Then the Emperor turned and pointed at Ling. "Behold, the one honest woman among you! My son will be best served by one with such integrity and purity in both heart and deed. Therefore, Ling is the one who shall marry my son!"

Think about it

- ❖ What qualities was the Emperor trying to discover? (Honesty; integrity; purity of heart and deed.)

- ❖ Do you think the Emperor's test was a good one? Why? (Yes. Because the women were unaware of the real test. Anyone can produce the 'goods', the necessary qualities for a time if they know what is being looked for.)

- ❖ Other glimpses of Ling's character were hidden in the story. Can you remember any? (She was hard working; she cared for her mother.)

The Gift of Values

Something to do

❖ Discuss with your older children what qualities they would be looking for in a wife or husband. Get them to write them down. Then read together the account of Samuel going to Jesse's home to anoint the next king. (1 Samuel 16:1-12) Note how even the prophet is impressed with Eliab's appearance. But the Lord says to him, "Do not consider his appearance or his height, for I have rejected him. The Lord does not look at the things man looks at. Man looks at the outward appearance, but the Lord looks at the heart." *1 Samuel 16:7 NIV*

So said...

❖ If you plant honesty, you will reap trust.
If you plant goodness, you will reap friends.
If you plant humility, you will reap greatness.
If you plant perseverance, you will reap victory.
If you plant consideration, you will reap harmony.
If you plant hard work, you will reap success.
If you plant forgiveness, you will reap reconciliation.
If you plant openness, you will reap intimacy.
If you plant patience, you will reap improvements.
If you plant faith, you will reap miracles.

BUT...

If you plant dishonesty, you will reap distrust.
If you plant selfishness, you will reap loneliness.
If you plant pride, you will reap destruction.
If you plant envy, you will reap trouble.
If you plant laziness, you will reap stagnation.
If you plant bitterness, you will reap isolation.
If you plant greed, you will reap loss.
If you plant gossip, you will reap enemies.
If you plant worries, you will reap wrinkles.
If you plant sin, you will reap guilt.

So be careful what you plant now. It will determine what you will reap tomorrow. The seeds you now scatter will make life worse or better - your life or the ones who will come after. Yes, someday, you will enjoy the fruits, or you will pay for the choices you plant today.

- "Honesty has a comeliness all of its own. It lights up the plainest face with a beauty that never fades." *R J Boom*

Words to live by

- "And the seed in the good ground, these are the ones who have heard the word in an honest and good heart, and hold it fast, and bear fruit with perseverance." *Luke 8:5 NIV* (N.B. Honesty is part of the good soil we need in our hearts.)

- "At this, the administrators and the satraps tried to find grounds for charges against Daniel in his conduct of government affairs, but they were unable to do so. They could find no corruption in him, because he was trustworthy and neither corrupt nor negligent. Finally these men said, "We will never find any basis for charges against this man Daniel unless it has Something to do with the law of his God." *Daniel 6:4, 5 NIV*

- "Finally brothers, whatever is true, whatever is noble, whatever is right, whatever is pure, whatever is lovely, whatever is admirable - if anything is excellent or praise-worthy - think about such things." *Philippians 4:8*

Dig deeper

- Listen to Tevya and Golda sing about their arranged marriage in *Fiddler on the Roof*. What countries still have arranged marriages? Discuss the pros and cons. Consider the quote, "In the West, marriages start in a hot pot and grow cold. In the East, an arranged marriage starts in a cold pot and grows warm."

- Watch the DVD *The Emperor's Club* with your older children. It's a powerful example of the difficult choices we may face with regard to honesty and cheating. Unfortunately, there are several parts in it that you'll want to fast forward. A shame really, but the movie is worth the trouble of checking out on www.pluggedinonline.com and then navigating around those parts.

Value Two

A POSITIVE ATTITUDE

Every day of our life we make choices. Lots of them. But few of them are as important as the attitudes we choose. Will we be angry or kind? Positive or negative? Will we be joyful or grumpy? The list is endless. Irritability is a choice. So is patience.

I will never forget the day my sister's two-year-old grizzled and whined. I wasn't a mother at this stage, and I couldn't believe it when Penny told her son to go into his room and only come out when he could be happy. What was she thinking? After all he was only two! Isaac cried and performed as Penny took him back to his room, and I thought to myself we wouldn't see him again for some time. I couldn't believe my eyes when he appeared in the kitchen, minutes later, all smiles and happiness. It was as if someone had pulled a magic switch inside his body.

Penny smiled at my astonishment and informed her ignorant single sister, "Sometimes all they need is a little help to change their attitude."

Boy, was that a lesson to me!

Charles Swindoll said, "The longer I live, the more I realize the impact of attitude on life. Attitude, to me, is more important than facts. It is more than the past, than education, than money, than circumstances, than failures, than successes, than what other people think or say or do. It is more important than appearance, giftedness or skill. It will make or break a company… a church… a home. The remarkable thing is we have a choice everyday regarding the attitude we will embrace for that day. We cannot change our past… we cannot change the fact that people will act in a certain way. We cannot change the inevitable. The only thing we can do is play on the one string we have, and that is our attitude… I am convinced that life is 10% what happens to me and 90% how I react to it. And so it is with you… we are in charge of our attitudes." What more can I say?

Don't Cry Over Spilt Milk

"If you choose to be angry for a minute, you lose sixty seconds of happiness."
Emerson

Holidays! I pulled the blankets up around my neck and revelled in the lazy feeling that washed over me. Today I would have a lie-in. Never mind that all the children were up and about, including Jacob, my one-year-old. He'd already had his morning feed and cuddle and was ready for some action with his siblings.

I lay in bed listening to the rabble in the dining room. Everyone was excited to have started the holidays. I started thinking about all the fun things I would do that day. The noise in the dining room grew louder. I tried to ignore it. Then I heard, "Mum! You'd better come here quickly!"

I jumped out of bed and ran into the dining room. I couldn't believe my eyes! There sat Jacob on top of our large round table. He had a bowl filled with at least ten crunched up Weet-Bix. On top of the Weet-Bix were the entire contents of the sugar bowl. But worst of all, he sat in a white puddle that covered the table and dripped off every side. The empty two litre container of milk lay beside him. I groaned as I watched milk drip onto all the cushion covers and down onto the floor. Our dog was happily licking from the ever increasing puddles. Jacob grinned at me, very proud of his achievements. He was holding the vegemite jar in his hand, and his face and hands were covered in a black sticky mess.

At this point I knew I had a choice. The morning could either quickly disintegrate into a misery for all of us, or else we could make it one of those moments we would never forget. It was up to me.

"Don't move him!" I yelled to the children as I ran back to my room to grab the camera.

Jacob beamed and smiled while we recorded the moment to show Daddy later. We were all laughing. It took me the next two hours to clean up the mess and wash all the milk sodden cushions, treading on them in the bath.

A disaster on the first day of the holidays, but one we will never forget. I suppose it serves me right for sleeping in!

What a joy it is when there's a cheerful atmosphere in the house. Everything seems easier. But oh boy, once grumbling and grumpiness get a hold, they spread like wildfire. If one member of the family wakes up in a bad mood, it can very easily set the thermometer for a chilly day. It takes a lot of hard work to lift the cloud of gloom. Everything seems such a chore. Grumpiness is like a thief that sneaks into our lives and robs us of all the joy and fun times we would have had throughout the day.

Now, it's easy enough to be cheerful when everything's going right, but what about when it seems like everything is going wrong?

The scary thing is, it's *Mum* who has the most influence on setting the cheerfulness level in the house! If we wake up and choose to be cheerful, generally the children and husband will follow suit. Now, I know that's not always the case, but especially if we are at home all day schooling the children, our own mood is the one that usually determines the general feel of the house. So, this lesson is as much for us as it is for our children!

Grumbling is a habit. So is cheerfulness. We can cultivate a grateful, cheerful heart, or we can choose to feed the habit of grumbling and complaining until it becomes a part of our everyday life.

The Bible has a lot to say about cheerfulness. Our memory verse for this subject is Proverbs 15:15. "A cheerful heart has a continual feast."

Who has the feast? The person with a cheerful heart. If you are cheerful, *you* will have a continual feast. *You* are the one who benefits. Life will be pleasant and good. Likewise, if you are miserable and grumpy, you will dine on old scraps and mouldy bread. Friends will come and go.

Life will be miserable.

Something to do

❖ Tell your children that today they are going to have all sorts of treats to eat. (This doesn't *have* to be sweets! You can easily make this activity healthy as well as fun!) Each time they get a treat they must quote Proverbs 15:15. Then ask each child to draw a happy face on a sticker. You draw one grumpy face. (When I did this, I didn't tell the children I'd drawn a grumpy face.) Tell them that they will only be allowed to have the treats if they are wearing a cheerful face sticker. Put all the stickers in a hat and ask each child to pull out a sticker and put it on their shirt.

Now… the child that pulls out the grumpy sticker is not going to be happy!

When we played this game, it just so happened that seven-year-old Milly, who had been grumpy all that morning, pulled out the appropriate sticker! Her face dropped. "Can I still have the treats, Mum?" she asked in a little voice.

"I'm sorry, darling," I said. "You only get to have a continual feast if you're wearing a cheerful face sticker. That's the rules." (That was hard to do, I might add!)

"But that's not fair!" she cried, as all the other children looked at me in astonishment. "I didn't get a choice!"

That was what I was waiting for! I stroked her little face and said, 'Well actually, you do have a choice, Milly. Do you want to trade your grumpy sticker for a happy face?"

She nodded vigorously and wiped her tears.

"Rip up the grumpy sticker then, darling," I said as I handed her a fresh sticker and the vivid marker. We were all grinning as she drew a very large smiley face on her sticker and slapped it on her chest.

The Gift of Values

That simple activity brought it home to all the children that we can choose whether we will be cheerful or grumpy - and that we ourselves are the ones who will either benefit from, or miss out on, all that each day has to offer.

- ❖ Now go and enjoy some treats together!
- ❖ Have some fun letting the children try to make the grumpiest faces they can.
- ❖ If you can find an old pair of glasses, put some dark paper over them and get each child to look through them. Explain that the habit of grumpiness affects what we see. Everything looks dark and gloomy.
- ❖ *What makes life 100%?* All ages will enjoy this. Get the children to write out all the letters of the alphabet. Make a code by writing the numbers 1 to 26 underneath the letters (A=1 etc). For practice, ask the children to work out the numerical value of a simple word, e.g. CAT = 3+1+20 = 24. Now get them to work out the following words: HARDWORK; KNOWLEDGE; ATTITUDE. It makes a good point! Hard work adds up to 98%; knowledge to 96%, but attitude scores a perfect 100%.

So said...

Years ago while foraging around in an antique shop, I discovered a tiny book called *Character and Conduct*. It is a collection of quotes by different great writers. On the subject of cheerfulness, it has a few good quotes.

- ❖ "The more cheerfulness, or good temper, is spent, the more of it remains." *Emerson*
- ❖ "Always laugh when you can; it is a cheap medicine. Cheerfulness is a philosophy not well understood. It is the sunny side of existence." *Byron*
- ❖ "Fortune will call at the smiling gate." *Japanese proverb*

- "Constant grumbling makes an ugly under-lip, a forehead wrinkled with frowning, and dull eyes that see nothing but grievances." *Mrs Ewing*

- "'How can you rejoice always?' asked one of the prisoners. 'Why, it is a grave sin not to do so. There's always good reason to rejoice! There is a God in heaven and in the heart. I had a piece of bread this morning - it was so good! Look now, the sun is shining. And so many here love me! Every day you do not rejoice is a day lost, my son. You will never have that day again.'" *Richard Wurmbrand*

- "Two men looked out through prison bars; one saw mud, the other stars." *Anon*

Words to live by

- "The joy of the Lord is your strength." *Nehemiah 8:10 NIV*

- "Though the fig tree does not blossom and there be no fruit on the vines; the produce of the olive fails and the fields yield no food: Though the flock be cut off from the fold and there be no herd in the stalls - YET I will rejoice in the Lord, I will joy in the God of my salvation." *Habakkuk 3:17,18 NASB*. (Get the children to count the number of 'negatives' in these verses. Six calamities, yet still the writer chooses to rejoice in his God.)

Dig deeper

- Read *A Christmas Carol* by Charles Dickens. Old Ebeneezer Scrooge was miserable and made everyone around him miserable - until he saw himself as he really was.

- Read the autobiography of Joni Erickson Tada, a young girl who became a quadriplegic in a diving accident. It tells of her struggles and how she eventually learns to rejoice in her wheelchair.

The Unfortunate Man

Let me tell you about an unfortunate man. When he was just twenty-two years old, he was fired from his job. He then began a business with a partner, but the business didn't make it. He tried politics, and finally managed to win a seat after being defeated twice. But then he promptly lost the seat. It was a dark time for him. When his girlfriend turned down his offer of marriage, and his political party passed him over, he suffered a nervous breakdown. Three more ventures into politics… three more defeats. Then at the age of fifty-one, after a history of memorable failures, he became President of the United States. His name? Abraham Lincoln.

Someone once said: "Two of the hardest things in life are failure and success." Teaching our children how to handle failure, and regard it not as an enemy, but as a potential friend, will be both a challenging and exciting task for us as parents. We need to make sure they know that even when they fail, they are not 'failures'.

All of us will taste the bitterness of failure at some point in our lives. But what we do with it, could determine the course of our lives.

How do we measure success and failure? So often it is by achievements, money or fame. These things are not the measure of a man!

I realised we needed to address the whole issue of the fear of failure when I found a beautiful picture drawn by five-year-old Katie screwed up in the rubbish. When I asked my little perfectionist why she had thrown it away instead of giving it to Nana as she had planned, she said it was no good - there was a mistake on it. On further examination, I discovered one tiny area where she had coloured over the line. Oh dear. Striving to do our best is one thing, but an unforgiving striving for perfection is another! As I thought about it, I realised that Kate was also the child who was reluctant to try something new. She would hang back and watch the other children try, and would only have a go herself when she felt fairly confident she could do it without failing. I realised she was scared of failure.

Over the next few weeks we looked at failure and our attitude towards it, and it was a wonderful learning time for all of us.

Think about it

- Is failure a bad thing? (Kate's answer to this was, "Not necessarily. It depends what you do with it." That's a good answer.)

- Why is it that failure destroys some people, yet others thrive and become stronger through it? (The secret is that they have learned to turn failure into their teacher, and their greatest defeats into learning experiences.)

- Why is the fear of failure such a negative thing, worse in fact than failure itself? (Eliza - "Because when you're afraid of failing, you never try. So if you would have got something, you don't get it!")

- What have you failed at? Succeeded at?

- Some failures and mistakes are easy to fix. You learn from them and get on with life. Others have more far-reaching consequences.

- Ask your children to think of some silly mistakes that are easily put right. (Jacob - "Putting your shoes on the wrong feet"; Milly - "Leaving the chicken coop door open." NB This could be more serious than it actually is, if Angel, our Jack Russell terrier, was less of an 'angel' than she is!)

The Gift of Values

- ❖ Then ask them to think of some that carry more permanent consequences. For example, a teenage boy drives his car while he is drunk. He makes an error of judgment and crashes into another car. The other driver is killed outright. What are some of the long-term consequences he will face? (A prison sentence; losing his licence; a guilty conscience.)

- ❖ A girl sleeps with her boyfriend. Six weeks later she discovers she is pregnant. God can and will forgive her sin if she asks Him to, but the consequences remain.

Something to do

❖ Next time you fail, ask these questions:

1. What have I learned? To learn you must be teachable. Ask God to help you discover the truths and lessons that are hidden within every failure.

2. How can I turn my failure into success? With persistence! Don't give up! Keep trying!

3. Who else has failed like this and how can they help me? The wonderful thing about the Bible is that it doesn't attempt to cover up human mistakes. Rather they are recorded for us, for our encouragement. Peter denied the Lord in a moment of trial, but later he became Peter, the rock. Can your children think of other examples?

4. Did I actually fail, or did I merely fall short of an unrealistically high goal? Get your children to write down both a realistic goal and an unrealistic goal. Discuss them. When we did this Katie wrote down, 'Realistic goal: I will pass Grade 5 piano this year. Unrealistic goal: I will become a concert pianist by next year.' Be careful when you do set goals. Do it prayerfully. And mums, we need to be aware of this when we set goals for our children. Make sure they are realistic ones; otherwise we are setting them up for failure and discouragement. Remind the children that God is not interested in whether we become famous or wealthy. He is interested in our character - who we are as people. He wants our love, not our successes. His love for us is not based on performance. He doesn't love us because we're a success. And He sure doesn't stop loving us when we fail.

The Gift of Values

Boom clip

When Josiah was eight years old, he asked for an apple just before dinner. I told him, "No, you can wait for dinner." He pleaded with me saying he was starving. I told him if he was that hungry he could have a carrot. He went to the fridge and chose a big carrot. He took a bite and then asked, "Can I trade the carrot for an apple?"

Good try, Joe! Full marks for creative thinking and not giving up!

Boom clip

I mixed up a double batch of peanut brownies and popped them in the oven, to be ready for afternoon tea. Just then the phone rang. It was my friend Robby. We chatted away, and the first I knew of a cooking disaster was when the smoke alarms shrilled and woke the baby. The whole kitchen was full of smoke. Choking, I grabbed the tray of black peanut brownies and ran outside. I pitched them over the fence into the paddock, where they smoked and smouldered away.

It took a long time for the smell of smoke to dissipate, and the whole time I felt increasingly annoyed at myself for forgetting the biscuits. I tried to put them out of my mind, but it wasn't until I'd gone back out and thrown them on the compost heap that I really moved past the whole episode. It was just a silly mistake, and one that was fairly easily rectified. All I lost were a few ingredients and time. Oh, and we didn't have afternoon tea.

So said...

- ❖ "Perfection addiction is just as quick a route to self-annihilation as a gun to the head." *Dr Anne Wilson Schaef*

- ❖ "Our doubts are traitors, and make us lose the good we oft might win, by fearing to attempt." *Shakespeare*

A Positive Attitude

- "One does not discover new lands without consenting to lose sight of the shore for a very long time." *Andre Gide*

- "Progress always involves risk. You can't steal second base and keep your feet on first." *Frederick Wilcox*

- "Anyone who has never made a mistake has never tried anything new." *Albert Einstein*

- "Failure is only a necessary step to success." (Henry Ford said this after he realised he had neglected to put a reverse gear in his first car.)

- "I would rather reach 90% of my potential with many mistakes, than reach 10% with a perfect score." *John Maxwell*

- "More people would learn from their mistakes if they weren't so busy denying them." *Harold Smith* (This is a biggie! We all have to learn to face up to our own mistakes and accept responsibility. Don't let your children try to shift blame either. That's exactly what Adam and Eve did in the garden after they disobeyed God.)

- "Give me a fruitful error anytime, full of seeds, bursting with its own corrections." *Vilfredo Pareto*

Words to live by

- "A righteous man falls seven times, but gets up again!" *Proverbs 24:16 NIV*

- "We get knocked down, but we get up again and keep going." *2 Corinthians 4:9 NIV*

- "Wash away all my iniquity and cleanse me from my sin… create in me a pure heart, O God, and renew a steadfast spirit within me." *Psalm 55:1, 10*

Dig deeper

- ❖ Watch the old black and white movie *It's a Wonderful Life* with your older children. The movie is about a man who feels he is a failure. At the end of the movie, an angel gives George a book with these words written inside the cover, "Remember, no man is a failure who has friends."

As an interesting aside, the movie itself appeared to be a failure. Although Capra said it was "the picture I waited all my life to make," it lost money on its initial release. Despite being nominated for Best Picture, Best Actor, Best Director, Best Sound and Best Film Editing, it failed to win a single Oscar. Critics rejected the film's sentimentality, and by the spring of 1947, *It's a Wonderful Life* appeared to be dead.

However, twenty-eight years after its release, someone forgot to renew the copyright for the film and it quietly slid into the public domain. This legal oversight was largely responsible for catapulting the movie to its current stature in film and cultural history. Television stations all over America realized they could show *It's a Wonderful Life* at no cost. Very quickly, the movie had reached millions of people. It seemed that people everywhere identified with George Bailey and his crisis of faith.

- ❖ Watch the movie *Cool Runnings*. There's an inspirational bit at the end where they crash their sled, but then pick it up and carry it over the finish line. Technically they had failed the race, but in fact, their courage made them, and their race, a huge success. Michael de Montaigne once said, "There are some defeats that are more triumphant than victories." Amen to that!

- ❖ Read about the Wright brothers in their early flying attempts. Failure had to be experienced before they finally were airborne. But was it actually failure?

A Positive Attitude

- Twelve publishers rejected Anne Montgomery's book, *Anne of Green Gables,* before it was accepted. Other authors could wallpaper a whole room with rejection slips before finally finding a publisher, and then having a best seller.

- Thomas Edison is one of the most inspiring examples of perseverance and optimism that I know. In the process of inventing the light bulb, he tried over two thousand experiments before it worked. A reporter asked him once how it felt to fail so often. He replied, "I never failed once. I invented the light bulb. It just happened to be a two thousand step progress."

Think about it! When would you have given up? After 387 attempts? 795? 1999? Edison also patented over one thousand inventions. Many of them were not his original ideas, but were those of other men who had cast them off as failures. When Edison was asked why he was so successful, he replied, "I start where other men leave off." Failure did not deter him.

The Gift of Values

Who Am I?

I am your constant companion.
I am your greatest helper
or your heaviest burden.
I will push you onward
or drag you down to failure.
I am completely at your command.
Half the things you do,
you might just as well turn over to me,
and I will be able to do them quickly and correctly.

I am easily managed; you must merely be firm with me.
Show me exactly how you want something done,
And after a few lessons I will do it automatically.
I am the servant of all great men.
And, alas, of all failures as well.
Those who are great, I have made great.

Those who are failures,
I have made failures.
I am not a machine,
Though I work with all the precision of a machine.
You may run me for profit, or run me for ruin;
It makes no difference to me.
Take me, train me, be firm with me

And I will put the world at your feet.
Be easy with me, and I will destroy you.
Who am I?

(Stop here and let your children guess.)

I am HABIT!

When people hear the word 'habit', ninety-five percent of them will immediately think of a negative habit. The fact is however, that good habits can have an incredibly powerful positive effect in our lives, just as negatives ones are terribly destructive. As parents, we have only a few short years to try and instill in our children's daily lives some good habits. Once they leave home, we haven't got the same window of opportunity. We won't be there to tell Johnny he's spent long enough on the computer or that it's time to go to bed. So, let's make the most of it. And of course, the sometimes painful truth is, we must teach by example. Let them see you reading your Bible in the morning. Let them hear you cheerfully greet them at the breakfast table. *Show* them how to set into place good habits.

Think about it

- ❖ Discuss with your children the paradox that something can have the potential to be so destructive, while at the same time also possess the potential to be 'our greatest helper'.

- ❖ How can we develop good habits? (There's no easy way. It takes commitment, consistency and determination before something becomes a habit.)

Something to do

❖ Give each of your children some paper and ask them to draw up two lists - one list of bad habits and the other of good habits. When they're finished, put all the ideas up on a whiteboard.

You may find like we did, that the children find it a lot easier and definitely more fun to identify their siblings' bad habits rather than their own! There was a lot of hilarity as we discussed some of these, with the younger ones teasing their big brother about sleeping in, their mother for biting her nails etc.

Some of the habits you write on the whiteboard may seem fairly insignificant, but when you examine them closely, you'll see they can have a profound effect in your life. Even the smallest adjustments are significant. The captain of the Titanic only needed to make a tiny adjustment to their course to save the ship.

Some of the many ideas we came up with were:

Bad Habits
Grumbling; lying; sleeping in; smoking; cheating; spending too long on the computer; biting your finger nails; drinking; saying mean things; not picking up your clothes; squinting; arguing; swearing; sniffing; frowning.

Good Habits
Reading your Bible each morning; prayer; saying thank-you; smiling; going to bed at a sensible time; listening; music practice; cheerfulness; brushing your teeth and putting your toothbrush away; keeping a journal - the list is endless.

❖ Now, get the children to think of one habit from each of their lists that they'll work on changing over the next fortnight. (Your children will love it if you try and do this as well.) Mums, make sure you help the little ones with a few prompts over the next few days. "Did you remember to hang up your towel, darling?" It won't take long before all they need is, "Did you re-…"

❖ You may like to offer a special award to any person who succeeds in breaking a bad habit, and establishing a good one. Present this at a special dinner. Aim to win an award yourself! This will be a huge encouragement to the children.

Boom clip

One of the greatest blessings in my life has been keeping a spiritual diary or journal. Earlier this year, Mum gave me a blank book to use as a diary, and in the front she had written a quote from Rick Warren: *"Your life is a journey that deserves a journal."*

So many of the things we're sure we'll never forget, slip from our minds like sand through our fingers. No wonder the Lord often instructed His people to write things down, and build monuments with stones of remembrance, *"lest they forget"*. Encourage your older children to begin a journal and write down anything they feel the Lord is saying to them. It will be a great blessing to them.

I love to read through my diary at year's end, and it's always a huge encouragement as I'm reminded of all the things the Lord has taught me. Another fun thing to do if you have a selection of old diaries, is have a 'day in history.' Go back and read your journal entries on a particular day over a number of years. I have also read from my diaries to the children - it gives them a very personal glimpse into my life. Needless to say, I choose the spots!

So said...

There are some great quotes below. Use them as discussion starters with your children. Even my young ones enjoy telling me what they think a quote means.

- "The chains of habit are too weak to be felt until they are too strong to be broken." *Samuel Johnson*
- "We are what we repeatedly do. Excellence, then, is not an act, but a habit." *Anon*
- "Bad habits are like a comfortable bed, easy to get into, but hard to get out of." *Anon*
- "Habits are cobwebs at first; cables at last." *Chinese Proverb*
- "Habit, if not resisted, soon becomes necessity." *St Augustine*
- "We first make our habits, and then our habits make us." *John Dryden*
- "It is easier to prevent bad habits than to break them." *Benjamin Franklin*
- "The unfortunate thing about this world is that good habits are so much easier to give up than bad ones." *Somerset Maugham*
- "The second half of a man's life is made up of nothing but the habits he has acquired during the first half." *Feodor Dostoevski*
- "Habit is the most imperious of all masters." *Goethe*
- "The will that yields the first time with some reluctance does so the second time with less hesitation and the third time with none at all, until presently the habit is adopted." *Henry Giles*
- "I will be a slave to no habit; therefore farewell tobacco." *Hosea Ballou*
- "To cease smoking is the easiest thing I ever did; I ought to know because I've done it a thousand times." *Mark Twain*

A Positive Attitude

- "Habit is a cable; we weave a thread of it each day, and at last we cannot break it." *Horace Mann*
- "Habit is either the best of servants or the worst of masters." *Nathaniel Emmons*
- "Habits are safer than rules; you don't have to watch them. And you don't have to keep them either. They keep you." *Frank Crane*

- "In truth, the only difference between those who have failed and those who have succeeded lies in the difference of their habits. Good habits are the key to all success. Bad habits are the unlocked door to failure. Thus, the first law I will obey, which precedes all others, is - 'I will form good habits and become their slave.'" *Og Mandino*
- "Sow an act… reap a habit; sow a habit… reap a character; sow a character… reap a destiny." *George D Boardman*
- "Ninety-nine percent of failures come from people who have the habit of making excuses." *George Washington*
- "Motivation is what gets you started. Habit is what keeps you going." *Jim Ryun*
- "Happiness is a habit - cultivate it." *Elbert Hubbard*
- "It's like magic. When you live by yourself, all your annoying habits are gone!" *Merrill Markoe*

Words to live by

- "Evening, morning and noon I cry out in distress and He hears my voice." *Psalm 55:17 NIV*
- "Three times a day he got down on his knees and prayed, giving thanks to God, just as he had done before." *Daniel 6:10 NIV*

Dig deeper

- ❖ Read the book *Run Baby Run* by Nicky Cruz and Jamie Buckingham with your older children. It tells of the destructive habits that ruled his life, and his dramatic conversion.

- ❖ Talk with your older children about drug and alcohol abuse. There are many good books on this subject in the public library.

- ❖ Watch the DVD *Walk the Line* with your older children. It's the inspiring story of Gospel singer Johnny Cash and his struggle with alcohol and drug addiction.

Value Three

COURAGE

The following advertisement was placed in London newspapers in 1900.

> MEN WANTED FOR HAZARDOUS JOURNEY. Small wages, bitter cold, long months of complete darkness, constant danger, safe return doubtful. Honour and recognition in case of success.
>
> *Ernest Shackleton*

Shackleton later said, "It seemed as though all the men in Great Britain were determined to accompany me, the response was so overwhelming."

There is something in the soul of man that wants a challenge. Even in the face of pain, hardship and trials, men and women tap into a God-given courage to do the unthinkable. Do they feel afraid? Yes. The brave or courageous person is not one who never feels afraid. Plato once said, "Courage is knowing what to fear."

The chief mate of the whaling ship in *Moby Dick* addressed his crew with these words, "I will have no man in my boat who is not afraid of the whale."

The Gift of Values

Courage, however, is not limited to facing physical dangers. Facing life's realities, its downs as well as its ups, is one kind of daily courage we all need to learn. Enduring sickness or grief requires courage. Learning to cope with disability demands a deep courage. It takes courage to go against the tide, and stand up for something you believe in. It takes great courage to be different.

In their book *Teaching Your Children Values*, Richard and Linda Eyre tell of the time they were trying to talk to their children about courage. They had been discussing the difference between the true courage of being a leader, resisting peer pressure and standing up for what you believe in, and the false courage of accepting dares and taking foolish risks. At that point, their eight-year-old daughter said, "Yeah - it takes real courage to be a chicken."

"What do you mean by that?" asked Richard.

"Well, I mean, like if kids are trying to get you to do something that you don't think is right - or it's really dangerous, and they're saying you're chicken, then it takes real courage to be a chicken and say, "Yeah, I'm a chicken."

Riot in the Prison

Adapted from *The Man with the Axe* by Dave and Neta Jackson

"Gladys Aylward! You must come quickly!" Loud pounding shook the gate of the Inn of the Eight Happinesses. Gladys dressed quickly and followed the man, her heart thumping. She could hear the terrible screams and cries coming from inside the local prison. It sounded like a riot. Why had she been summoned by the Mandarin? She saw him standing with the governor of the prison outside the huge gates. She approached them and bowed respectfully.

"Thank goodness you have come!" said the governor. "You must go in and stop the riot!"

Gladys's eyes grew wide. "Me? Me go in there? Why don't you send in your soldiers?"

"Impossible!" cried the governor. "My soldiers would surely be killed by these murderers and thieves!"

Gladys listened in unbelief. "But if I go in there, I too will be killed."

"Oh no," replied the governor. "You tell our people that there is a God who lives inside you. If that be true, he will protect you."

Gladys's mouth went dry. He was serious! He wasn't making fun of her. The two men stared at her, waiting for her answer. In an instant she knew. If she doubted God's protection now, she may as well return to England. China was no place for her.

She took a deep breath to try and calm her pounding heart. "Alright," she said. "I will go in. Open the gate."

As the great doors swung open, Gladys saw a terrible sight. Wounded prisoners lay all over the compound, moaning and crying. The bodies of the dead lay everywhere. Men were chasing each other with machetes and screaming like madmen. Gladys felt the blood drain from her face. A large man ran straight towards her, his bloodied axe high above his head.

Gladys was so terrified she couldn't move. Then suddenly the prisoner stopped a metre in front of her and stared in amazement. What was a tiny woman doing here? He stood there speechless, his axe hanging at his side. One by one, the other prisoners caught sight of her and stared in astonishment.

Then Gladys found her tongue. "Give me that axe!" she snapped, holding out her hand.

Without a word, the man handed her the axe. Gladys looked at the prisoners. They were filthy and dressed in rags. Their ribs stuck out in emaciated bodies, and they shivered with cold. Suddenly all her fear evaporated. In its place was a deep compassion. "I have been sent in here to find out why you are rioting." Her voice was clear and strong.

No one spoke. Then a young man stepped forward. "My name is Feng," he said. "We are hungry and cold and have nothing to do day after day. That is why we fight."

Gladys looked around them. They were like caged animals, with little food and no work to pass the hours. "If you will promise to stop fighting, and will care for the wounded and bury the dead, I will speak to the governor for you," she said.

The prisoners agreed. As the little woman stepped out from the prison, both the Mandarin and the governor bowed to her with respect.

"These men must be allowed to work, so they can earn money and buy food," she said. "They must regain their self-respect."

The governor nodded.

"And I shall be here every day to ensure you carry this out!" Gladys added, her eyes flashing.

True to her word, Gladys began visiting the prisoners every day. She read them stories from the Bible and taught them basic hygiene. Two old looms were donated to the prison and Gladys begged yarn from the local merchants. She also managed to get an old miller's wheel so that the prisoners could grind their own grain. Gladys even taught the men how to breed rabbits to sell. Within a few months of the riot, the prisoners were all warmly dressed and eating well. From that time on, she was called Ai-weh-deh - 'virtuous one'. Everyone in the district knew her as the 'riot-stopper', a brave and virtuous woman.

Think about it

- ❖ Was Gladys courageous? Was she also afraid?
- ❖ Where does courage come from? (A 'knowing' that God is with us and that He is greater than all our adversaries.)
- ❖ Why did Gladys decide she must go in? (It would be a clear demonstration to all watching, that the God she spoke of was true.)

Something to do

- ❖ Act out the story of Daniel in the lion's den *(Daniel 6)*. Like Gladys, he also had a choice of whether or not to 'go in' to a dangerous place. If he had obeyed the law, he wouldn't have had to face the punishment. But like Gladys, he found the courage to 'go in.' And God was glorified through his courage.

So said...

- ❖ "Courage is a special kind of knowledge; the knowledge of how to fear what ought to be feared and how not to fear what ought not to be feared." *David Ben-Gurion*
- ❖ "Courage is fear that has said its prayers." *Karle Wilson Baker*
- ❖ "Never take counsel of your fears." *Andrew Jackson*

The Gift of Values

- "Heroism is the brilliant triumph of the soul over the flesh - that is to say over fear: fear of poverty, of suffering, of sickness, of isolation, and of death. There is no serious piety without heroism. Heroism is the dazzling and glorious concentration of courage." *Amiel's Journal*

- "Without Christ, not one step; but with Him - anywhere!" *David Livingstone*

Words to live by

- "For God has not given to us a spirit of fear, but of power and of love and of a sound mind." *2 Timothy 1:7 NKJV*

- "When I am afraid, I will trust in Thee. In God whose word I praise, in God I have put my trust; I shall not be afraid." *Psalm 56:3, 4 NASB*

- "Be strong and courageous, do not fear or be dismayed because of the king of Assyria, nor because of all the multitude which is with him; for the one with us is greater than the one with him. For with him is only an arm of flesh, but with us is the Lord our God to help us and fight our battles." *2 Chronicles 32:7, 8 NASB*

- "For we are powerless before this great multitude who are coming against us; nor do we know what to do, but our eyes are on Thee." *2 Chronicles 20:12 NIV* Read the chapter to get the whole story of fear and courage and trust in God.

Dig deeper

- Watch the video *Shackleton* with your older children.

- Watch the video *The Inn of the Six Happinesses*, starring Ingrid Bergman as Gladys. It is a wonderful portrayal of her life in China. Probably suitable for 10 years and up.

❖ Read the book and/or watch the movie *The Hiding Place*, which tells the story of Corrie Ten Boom, a Dutch woman who was imprisoned in Ravensbrück concentration camp for hiding Jews during World War II.

❖ Read *The Courage of Sarah Noble* with your younger children. It tells the story of a young girl who goes with her father to the frontier to prepare a new home for their family.

❖ Read *The Matchlock Gun* by Walter D. Edmonds with your younger children. It's the true story of a boy who protects his mother and sister from Indians in the Hudson valley.

❖ Read *Owl Moon* by Jane Yolen with your young children. The shadows in the woods are very black. When you go owling, you have to be brave, even when you go with your father.

❖ Read about Harriet Tubman, a black woman who helped slaves escape to the northern state on the Underground Railroad.

❖ Read *The Door in the Wall* by Marguerite de Angeli. It is the story of a boy left crippled by an illness, who learns the purpose of life in medieval London. There are some great quotes and truths in this book. Also available is a study guide by Andrew Clausen, prepared for Grades 4 - 6 - a great way to dig deeper into this wonderful story.

❖ Watch *The Lion, The Witch and The Wardrobe* with the family. At one point Susan tells Peter, "Just because someone in a red coat gives you a sword, it doesn't make you a hero!"

❖ Watch the movie *Apollo 13* with your teens. It showcases courage and determination in the face of adversity. (Caution: it does contain a number of profanities. Check it out on www.pluggedinonline.com.)

❖ Watch the movie *Iron Will* with your children. (Probably suitable for 10 years and up.) It tells the story of a seventeen-year-old who enters a 522-mile-long dog sled race, in the hopes of winning the $10,000 prize so he can help his mother pay off the family's debts.

Orange in a Sea of Grey

Driving home from a concert one day we went past a new subdivision. I said to the children, "Look at that! All the roofs are grey. They're all the same. It looks like a grey sea."

A few moments later we drove over a hill, and there was one orange roof amongst all the grey ones. It stood out like a sore thumb. Straight away, I began to write a little ditty:

Dare to be different,
Orange in a sea of grey.
Dare to stand out from the crowd,
Do things a different way.

As I drove into church that night, I thought further about what we'd seen and realized that the colours were perfect for the analogy.

Think about it

- ❖ Ask the children what colours you have to mix to get grey. (White and black.)

- ❖ What might that speak of? (Compromise, mixture.)

- ❖ Ask them to think about a characteristic of the colour orange. If they can't think of anything, ask them what colour the road workers wear. Why do they wear orange? (Because it is very visible.)

- ❖ How does this analogy apply to us? (God wants us to be like the orange roof - visible and with lives that are very different from those lived by unbelievers.)

- ❖ Ask the children for some examples of being 'orange in a sea of grey.' (Not cheating in exams; not living with your boyfriend/girlfriend; not being self-absorbed; not cheating in your tax forms.)

Something to do

- For a week play 'Spot the Orange'. We have had lots of fun doing this, and usually each sighting is accompanied with the quote, "Orange in a sea of grey!" You could even make that a prerequisite. Some of our finds have included road signs; road markings; harbour bridge signs; road worker jackets; bush walk markers (orange triangles on trees); road cones; indicator lights; traffic light poles… the list goes on and on.

- Make a visit to a second-hand shop and see if you can each find a bright orange t-shirt to wear. It may not suit you, but it will be a great reminder and you'll have a lot of fun doing it.

Boom clip

Yesterday we celebrated Jacob's sixth birthday. A fierce storm blew in just as we had to drive some of his friends home after the party. We were drenched just getting into the car. When we left, the other children were sliding around the front lawn in huge puddles!

We dropped Ben home first and then drove off down the country road. We hadn't gone far before Genevieve realized she had left her new sunglasses at Ben's house. I told her we'd turn around and go back. However, in navigating my three point turn on the narrow road, I managed to get stuck in a ditch. It was quite easy really.

I felt decidedly vulnerable sitting there, with the back wheels in a ditch full of rain water and the front of the van sticking out across the road. The rain was pelting down and visibility was very poor. I hoped no cars would come racing along the road. Praise the Lord for cell phones.

"Just as well the back of the van is bright orange, eh kids?" I said as we waited for help to arrive. The words were out of my mouth before I'd even thought about them. But as we sat there with our orange hazard lights flashing, we realized that we had just found another good example of 'orange in a sea of grey.'

So said...

- "It is curious - curious that physical courage should be so common in the world, and moral courage so rare." *Mark Twain*

- "Courage is not limited to the battlefield or the indianapolis 500 or bravely catching a thief in your house. The real tests of courage are much quieter. They are the inner tests, like remaining faithful when nobody's looking, like enduring pain when the room is empty, like standing alone when you're misunderstood." *Anon*

- "Have the courage to say no. Have the courage to face the truth. Do the right thing because it is right. These are the magic keys to living your life with integrity." *W. Clement Stone*

- A verse from Phoebe Cary's poem *Our Heroes* talks about having the moral courage to do what is right, despite the opinions of the crowd.

Our Heroes

Here's a hand to the boy who has courage
To do what he knows to be right;
When he falls in the way of temptation,
He has a hard battle to fight.
Who strives against self and his comrades
Will find a most powerful foe.
All honour to him if he conquers.
A cheer for the boy who says, "NO!"

Words to live by

- "Do not conform any longer to the pattern of this world (don't let the world squeeze you into its mould), but be transformed by the renewing of your mind. *Romans 12:2 NIV*

- ❖ "Do everything without grumbling or complaining, that you may become blameless and pure, children of God without fault in a crooked and depraved generation, in which you shine as stars in the universe, holding forth the Word of life." *Philippians 2:14–16 NIV.* (Amazing! Even such a little thing as not complaining can set us apart and cause us to shine like stars in a dark world.)

Dig deeper

- ❖ Watch the Veggie tales movie *Rack, Shack and Benny*.
- ❖ Watch the movie *Chariots of Fire* with your older children. It tells the inspiring true story of Eric Liddell, the Scottish runner who refused to compete on a Sunday.
- ❖ Watch the movie *Bonhoeffer* (mature audiences). It is a true story of courage, love and sacrifice. Dietrich Bonhoeffer spoke out against Hitler's regime and has become a symbol of civil courage and indomitable faith.
- ❖ Read the story of Daniel and his three friends, Shadrach, Meshach and Abed-nego in Daniel Chapter 3. When first taken as captives to Babylon, they refused to eat the king's rich food. That was an act of moral courage. It prepared them for the great test later in their lives when they were commanded to bow down before the golden idol. Their courage was grounded in their God whom they served. They dared to stand out from the crowd.

Just a thought here. Never underestimate the power and strength of godly friends. James Dobson did a survey with college students that clearly demonstrated this. A group of students were told to choose an obviously wrong answer when asked a question. Only one person was not in the loop.

The Gift of Values

When he saw all the others choosing the wrong answer, his own judgment was swayed and he threw his lot in with them. Time and time again this happened. In fact, 75 percent of all the young people tested behaved in this way. Only 25 percent had the courage to take their stand against the group, even when the majority was obviously wrong. But then they changed the set up. This time, one person in the group was told to vote for the right answer. The results were amazing. Just having one other person who was willing to vote against the majority, greatly increased the chances of the other person finding the courage to vote for what he felt was right. Proverbs 13:20 says, "He who walks with the wise will himself be wise, but the companion of fools will suffer harm."

☙

A Foolish Dare

My friend Margie and I sprinted along the jungle path. The rain stung our skin and the loud cracks of thunder hurt our ears.

"Come on!" I yelled back to my twin sister, Penny, who ran behind us. Double trouble our parents called us. Papua New Guinea was the best place in the world for girls like us. Dense jungle surrounded the mission station and swarmed with adventure.

Poita, our blue heeler dog, ran beside us, tail between her legs. She hated thunderstorms. But we loved them!

We reached the bridge and looked down at the swollen river. It flowed fast and rough, its waters churned up by the heavy rain.

"Shouldn't we wait till the lightning stops?" asked Margie.

"Nah," I said. "It's ok. We do it all the time." I didn't tell her that Dad had forbidden us to swim during a thunderstorm. Penny looked as if she was going to say something but I silenced her with a look.

"Okay, let's all jump at the same time," I suggested.

Margie took a step back. "I don't really want to jump, Rose. I'll watch you and Penny do it."

"Scared are you?" I scoffed. "It's only twelve feet down. Don't be a baby. Come on, we'll hold hands." I grabbed her hand and pulled her towards the edge. Just then forked lightning lit up the jungle. I quickly dropped her hand and we all covered our ears. The crack of thunder shook the bridge. Poita yelped, and bolted back to the mission station.

Margie had shrunk back from the edge again. "I really don't want to jump," she whispered.

"Don't be a sissy," I said. "You can be in the middle. Come on, I dare you!" I pulled her back to the edge. "I'll count to three, then we'll jump together. One, two, three!"

We jumped. I lost hold of Margie's hand just before I hit the water.

The Gift of Values

The rain pelted my face when I surfaced. It was hard to see anything. I made for the bank and found Penny.

"Cool eh?!" I shouted above the rain. "Where's Margie?"

Penny looked nervous. "I don't know, Rose. I haven't seen her."

I squinted into the rain. Nothing. Margie had disappeared.

Suddenly Penny grabbed my arm. "There, Rose! Look!"

Margie was floating face down in the river, about ten metres downstream. My mouth went dry. I tried to shout but the words wouldn't come.

We ran along the bank and dived into the swirling river.

We reached her at the same time. I grabbed her hair and yanked her face out of the water. Penny got hold of her arms and turned her onto her back. She felt so heavy. My legs were like jelly, and I was fighting to get a deep breath. What if she was dead? What if she'd been struck by lightning? I was sick with fear.

At last we reached the side and hauled Margie up the slippery bank. She lay in the mud, still and pale. Penny and I sat beside her, gasping for breath. We didn't know what to do. Then I vaguely remembered something I'd heard at a Red Cross camp.

"Quick! Help me roll her on her side."

As we struggled to move her, Margie suddenly heaved and vomited up heaps of dirty water. She was alive! Quickly Penny and I sat her up and rubbed her arms. She was shaking all over. I grabbed a towel and wrapped it round her shoulders.

"I fainted," she said, her teeth chattering.

I could taste the tears that streamed down my face with the rain. "I'm so sorry, Margie. I'm sorry I bullied you. I'll never, ever do it again."

I looked at my double trouble twin. Boy, we were going to be in for it tonight when Dad found out. But I knew we deserved whatever punishment he gave us. This time I had really learned my lesson. Dares can be dangerous.

Think about it

- Have you ever been dared to do something that is dangerous or wrong? Have you perhaps dared someone else?

- Can you say no?

- Do you have the courage to be a chicken?

- Consider Daniel *(Daniel 6)*. He was given a 'dare' by the evil men in the kingdom - *we dare you to keep on praying!* Now, this is one dare that can be taken up! But facing the lions will take more courage than jumping off a bridge!

Something to do

- Work out a plan of what you could say next time someone says, "I dare you!" Brainstorm together of creative ways you can say, "No!"

- A fun thing to do is to create some scenarios the children can act out. Only disclose the plot to one child and make the other one think on his feet.

  For example, hand one child a piece of paper with the following scenario written out.
  You are playing with your friend. Tell him your parents are out tomorrow night and he's allowed to come over for the evening to watch a video. Then you must let slip that you've going to show a different video than the one you told your parents about. Indicate that it's a movie that they would not approve of.
  Now call in the other child and let them play it out. It will be interesting to see how the other child responds - what he comes up with by way of excuse.

  Your children may be embarrassed at the start to do this sort of thing - mine were. But after a few goes, they get the hang of it, and it really helps them to get some strategies in place.

Here are some great tips I heard about how to act when you encounter negative peer pressure. Some of them will work in certain scenarios, some will be better in others.

1. Say 'NO' in less than 30 seconds. Don't wait any longer than that. Say it no more than twice and then leave the scene if the pressure is not off. This point applies to every scenario. Don't hang around!
2. Speak in a firm voice. No weak phrases.
3. Avoid debate. This is where the 30 second rule comes in.
4. There are many ways you can cope in a difficult situation. The following are some ideas: Simply say no; leave the scene (Joseph fled!); ignore the peer; make an excuse; change the subject; suggest a better idea; return the challenge. Have a run through with your children with all the ideas above; let them get used to using them. Practice. And remember the 30 second rule! They must say "no" within that time frame.

Words to live by

❖ Jesus was 'dared' to do something by Satan. While fasting in the wilderness, Satan appeared to Jesus and tempted Him. "And he led him to Jerusalem and set Him on a high pinnacle of the temple, and said to Him, 'If you are the Son of God, cast yourself down from here; for it is written, "He will give His angels charge concerning You to guard You," and "On their hands they will bear You up, lest You strike Your foot on a stone."' And Jesus answered and said to him, 'It is said, "You shall not force a test on the Lord your God."'" *Luke 4:9-12 NIV*

❖ "For the grace of God that brings salvation has appeared to all men. It teaches us to say *'NO!'* to ungodliness and worldly passions, and to live self-controlled, upright and godly lives in this present age." *Titus 2:11 NIV* (When we memorized this scripture, the children loved to yell out the "NO!")

So said...

- "If fifty million people say a foolish thing, it is still a foolish thing." *Anatole France*

- "Hermits have no peer pressure." *Steven Wright*

- "When the loud voice of peer pressure shouts in your ear, tune in to the quiet, gentle voice that whispers in your heart." *R J Boom*

- "Most teenagers respect a guy or a girl who has the courage to be his own person, even when being teased. An individual with this kind of courage often becomes a leader." *James Dobson*

Dig deeper

- Read or watch *Anne of Green Gables*. Anne accepts a dare by Josie Pye to walk the ridgepole of a house. She falls and sprains her ankle. Anne clearly demonstrates the pride that is often associated with not being able to turn down a dare.

☙

The Gift of Values

Flynn of Thrim

*Evil's banishment, tyranny's defeat
When the bearer of courage thrice faces the beast*

High in the mountains, above the tiny village of Thrim was a cave. Deep in the dark cave shone a strange light. On the blackest of nights, when the stars hid behind the clouds, its faint eerie glow could be seen by the villagers in the valley below. It was the shadow over their hearts, the blight on their happiness. But legend had it, that one day from among them, a deliverer would arise, who would dare to climb the mountain and face the dragon.

Graub was bored. No valiant knights to fight, no fearless warriors to sizzle. And he was sick of counting his treasure. In fact he was altogether sick of his tedious existence. He needed a challenge. Something to make his nostrils flare and his claws tingle. It was time.

The next morning the villagers of Thrim heard a *thrum, thrum, thrum* in the mist. They gathered at the well and strained their eyes. Suddenly a huge shape soared above them. Children screamed and their mothers covered their faces with their aprons. The menfolk clutched at their daggers. Graub circled once then opened his claws. An oblong shape fell to the earth with a thud. Then with a slice of his scaled tail, Graub was gone. The villagers ran over to the object and stared. It was gold. A large nugget of the purest gold they had ever seen. And stamped on both sides was a large 'T'. It was the ancient Thrimmin gold.

A meeting was called that night.

"We can escape it no more," declared Boris the Brave. "The time has come. Graub has issued his challenge."

Courage

The womenfolk fidgeted and the men kept their eyes on the floor. Only one set of eyes found Boris's. Clear and blue, they met his gaze, steady and confident. Boris gave a small shake of his head. But Flynn's voice rang out loud and clear. "I will go."

Everyone spun around to look at the slight form of the blacksmith's son. He was thirteen years old and as thin as a reed, but some said the blacksmithy's fire burned in his heart.

"I will go,' he said again, and there was something in his quiet voice that made the elders nod.

He set off the next morning before the sun had gilded the hills. He took with him some bread and cheese wrapped in a cloth, his mother's pearl inlaid mirror, and his blacksmith's hammer. It was noon by the time he reached the dragon's lair. He stood at the edge of the clearing and tried to catch his breath.

"So, the men of Thrim send a boy," hissed the dragon.

Flynn spun around to see Graub pacing silently behind him, his scales glittering green and gold in the sun. He said nothing but kept his eyes on the dragon.

"Very well," sneered Graub, "let the contest begin."

He led the way to the mouth of the cave then spun around and faced the forest. With a terrible snarl he roared, "What can burn as hot as Graub?" And he opened his terrible jaws and a jet of white hot fire scorched the earth and burst into flame two towering pines.

Flynn stepped forward. He walked straight up to the smoking nostrils of the dragon, unbuttoned his shirt and bared his chest. Then fixing his young eyes on the hooded green slits of Graub, he cried out, "Flynn of Thrim burns hotter than Graub!"

Raw courage burned like fire in the thin chest of the boy. At the sight of it, Graub snarled and slunk back into his cave. "Follow me," he hissed.

The Gift of Values

Flynn blinked as he entered the damp darkness of the dragon's lair. Way ahead he could see a golden glow that seemed to throb with life. A strange humming noise reached him. It was Graub chanting.

"Beautiful. Beautiful. Graub's treasure's beautiful. What can match the beauty of Graub's gold?"

Flynn gasped. He stood at the door of an enormous cavern. Inside, a million lights blinked at him. Rubies, sapphires, emeralds and gold - gold everywhere. The gold of Thrim.

Graub clattered beside him. "So, Flynn of Thrim, now show me your treasure."

Carefully Flynn pulled out his mother's pearl inlaid mirror. He held it up before his face. "Come, Graub. See what you can see."

The dragon slunk behind him and his evil eyes darted at the mirror.

"They say I have my mother's eyes," whispered Flynn.

Graub could not look away. He remembered those eyes. Honest. Guileless. True. With a swipe of his claws, he smashed the mirror onto the bed of brilliant stones.

A deep rumble began to fill the cave. Graub tipped back his awful head and roared, "I am Graub! There is no sound more terrible than Graub!" Then his enormous jaws opened and Graub roared - a terrible, hideous roar.

Down in the valley, the villagers of Thrim trembled and crossed their hearts.

The dragon shook himself and slowly spun his great head to stare at Flynn. "What says you, Flynn of Thrim?" he snarled.

Flynn stared at the ugly face of the dragon for a moment, then turned his back and picked his way over the jewels to the farthest corner of the cave.

Taking out his blacksmith's hammer, he cried out in a loud voice, 'Flynn of Thrim fears not Graub!" And he swung with all his might and smashed his hammer against the wall of the cave. Again and again he struck… louder and louder, until the very mountain awoke and rumbled and roared. The shriek of

Courage

the dragon was drowned out as Flynn struck again and again, and the echo of truth spun around the cave - "… fears not Graub, fears not Graub."

Down in the valley, the villagers raised their heads with hope, and every eye watched as a dark form flapped and circled up, up, up and far away from the mountains of Thrim.

Think about it

- ❖ What were the three tests? (The hottest fire; the greatest treasure; the loudest roar.)

- ❖ Discuss the quote, 'Courage burns the strongest in an honest heart.'

- ❖ Was Flynn courageous?

- ❖ Do we need courage today? Why? There aren't any dragons to fight. (Because there are 'other' dragons we need to fight.) What could be some 'modern-day' dragons?

- ❖ When Flynn looked in the mirror, what did it show? (An honest heart, a clear conscience, guilelessness.) Ask the children who they can think of in the Bible that showed a similar courage to Flynn. Most will think of David facing Goliath. This is a great story for acting out as a skit. Even my older children get involved in these re-enactments with zest.

I recently heard a funny story about a family acting out the story of David and Goliath. Dad came in shaking his spear and taunting David. "Are you a coward?!" he roared.

Now little David may not have understand the word, but he recognized the challenge in the giant's voice. He threw out his chest, stood as straight as he could, and shouted back, "YES, I AM!!"

- ❖ Other potential ideas to explore in the Bible would be Queen Esther risking her life to plead for the Jews before the king. Mordecai told her that "perhaps she had come to the kingdom for such a time as this." We

The Gift of Values

will all need courage to fulfil our destiny; Elijah facing the prophets of Baal and King Ahaz; Nathan taking God's word of judgment to King David; Shadrach, Meshach and Abed-nego refusing to bow down before the golden idol; Daniel continuing to pray under threat of being thrown to the lions. As Hebrews 11:32-34 *(*NIV) says, "And what more shall I say? For time will fail me if I tell of Gideon, Barak, Samson, Jephthah, of David and Samuel and the prophets, who by faith conquered kingdoms, obtained promises, shut the mouths of lions, quenched the power of fire, escaped the edge of the sword, from weakness were made strong, became mighty in battle, put foreign armies to flight."

The examples are endless.

Something to do

- ❖ Get the children to draw a picture of Graub and Flynn fighting.

- ❖ Make some wooden swords and stage a challenge between some knights and a dragon. Remind the children not to get *too* carried away with their swords though - we had one child get so excited she whacked her knight brother very hard with her sword. Even brave knights have been known to cry sometimes!

- ❖ Read the story of David and Goliath in 1 Samuel 17, and find out what David took with him to face his 'dragon.' (A stick, a slingshot, five smooth stones, and the name of the Lord of Hosts.)

- ❖ The enemy of our souls, Satan, is also known as the dragon *(Rev 20:2).* We face him with the sword of the Spirit which is the Word of God. We also have a shield of faith and the helmet of salvation *(Eph 6:10-17).* You could do a study on putting on the whole armour of God.

- ❖ Read what happens to Satan, the dragon, in Revelation 20.

So said...

- "Promise me you'll always remember: You're braver than you believe, and stronger than you seem, and smarter than you think." *Christopher Robin to Pooh*

- "Courage is resistance to fear, mastery of fear - not absence of fear." *Mark Twain*

- "Courage is knowing what to fear." *Plato*

- "Courage is almost a contradiction in terms. It means a strong desire to live taking the form of readiness to die." *G K Chesterton*

Words to live by

- "Just as I have been with Moses, I will be with you; I will not fail you or forsake you. Be strong and courageous, for you shall give this people possession of the land which I swore to their fathers to give them." *Joshua 1:5, 6 NIV*

- Joshua had been chosen to fulfil a great task. The reason why he could be courageous was because of God's promise to be with him. We are not courageous in our own might, but in the knowledge of the Lord's promises and presence.

- "Wait for the Lord; be strong, and let your heart take courage; yes, wait for the Lord." *Psalm 27:14 NIV*

- "These things I have spoken to you, that in Me you may have peace. In the world you have tribulation, but take courage; I have overcome the world." *John 16:33 NIV* (Note the words *"take courage"*. It is there for the taking. Jesus offers us courage. When we choose to believe His words we are choosing to take courage.)

Dig deeper

- Read *Pilgrim's Progress* by John Bunyan together. Comic forms are available for little children, and abridged editions for early readers. When Pilgrim reaches the house of the Interpreter he is given a set of armour to wear and then goes out and faces the dragon, Apollyon.

- Read *The Hunting of the Last Dragon* by Sheryl Jordan with your older children. It has some great analogies in it.

- Another great family read is *The Great and Terrible Quest* by Margaret Lovett. This story centres on a young boy, an orphan, who is growing up in the care of a cruel man. The young boy helps a wounded stranger, an act of generosity and kindness, and saves the wounded stranger from his cruel guardian. The stranger is suffering memory loss but must complete a very important quest to save their country. The young boy sets off to help the old man with his quest. It's a wonderful book, exciting and vivid, with a great ending. It is available from Sonshine Curriculum.

- Read the story of *Chicken Little* with your younger children. Mark Twain once said that he had known a lot of troubles in his life, and most of them never happened. Poor Chicken Little feared the sky was falling - how wrong she was!

- Most of the biographies of Christian missionaries have stories of courage and bravery. Some examples are *God's Smuggler* by Brother Andrew; *A Prisoner and Yet* and *The Hiding Place* by Corrie Ten Boom; *Granny Brand* by Dorothy Clarke Wilson.

- Read *The House of Sixty Fathers* by Meindert DeJong. It tells the dramatic account of a Chinese boy during the Japanese war.

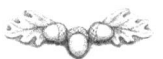

Value Four

DILIGENCE

Diligence. It has a certain ring about it - and not always a pleasant one. Maybe that's because it makes us think of responsibility? Or maybe because we know it equates to work? And yet diligence can offer us the world!

It would be good to ask your children what this word means, and then look it up together in the dictionary. The Oxford dictionary defines 'diligent' as being *"careful and persevering in carrying out tasks or duties."*

One of my worst classes during high school was Latin. I'm not quite sure why I took it for four years. I must say though, you can get a great understanding of some of our English words by looking at their Latin derivative. The word 'diligent' actually comes from a Latin word 'diligere' which means 'to value'. Now that puts a really good slant on it. We are only diligent about something if we value it. We are diligent about exercise and healthy eating if we value our health; we are diligent in music practice if we realise the value of being able to play an instrument; we are diligent in relationships if we realise how important friendships and family are. To be diligent in something we must value it.

One of the greatest gifts we can give our children is helping them develop diligence in their lives. We do this by ensuring they have responsibilities and chores, and by making sure they fulfil them. One of the foundational truths about diligence is that it is lived out in the small decisions, the little moments of each day. Just the other week, I was talking to an employer who made this comment. "I would rather employ someone who faithfully turns up to work each morning, than the top student from University. Nowadays, it's hard to find someone that you can count on to come to work every day."

However, diligence doesn't just apply to physical work. We are encouraged to "work out our salvation with fear and trembling." *Philippians 2:12 NIV.*

We've probably all experienced the frustration of feeling that our children just aren't listening properly during family devotions. Maybe we feel that although they are sitting there, the words are going in one ear and out the other.

One of the truths we need to somehow get across to them is that *they* are responsible for the state of their own hearts. Even very young children need to be taught this. Mum and Dad can teach and talk and be godly examples to them ad infinitum, but ultimately it will be their choice whether they walk with the Lord or not. We cannot make our children godly. We can only present them with truth and life, and pray that they will choose wisely.

Our children need to learn to be diligent in their spiritual life. The following passage of Scripture clearly illustrates that we all need to apply diligence to grow in the faith.

"But also for this very reason, giving all diligence, add to your faith goodness; and to your goodness, knowledge; and to your knowledge, self-control; and to self-control, perseverance; and to perseverance, godliness; and to godliness, brotherly kindness; and to brotherly kindness, love. For if you possess these qualities in increasing measure, they will keep you from being ineffective and unproductive in your knowledge of our Lord Jesus Christ." *2 Peter 1:5-10 NIV.*

There you have it. There's no way around it. If we want to grow in our knowledge of Jesus and be used by Him, we need to be diligent.

As my pastor used to say, "The whole world lies at the feet of a diligent man."

☙

The Elephant's Trunk

When the jeep pulled into Chitwan National Park, Nepal, I couldn't wait to get out and explore. A Nepali showed me to my small hut which was sparsely decorated with a small chest of drawers, a bed with a mosquito net, and a chair. I planned to stay there for several days and go on an elephant trek, and hopefully see some tigers and rhinos.

After a quick drink, I went outside to join the other tourists for a guided tour around the compound. Our guide took us to a flat area just outside the buildings where ten or twelve elephants were tethered. We all clicked away with our cameras, excited to be so close to these huge, majestic animals. It felt quite different to seeing the elephants in a zoo. Then our guide asked us a question. "What do you think these elephants are most afraid of?"

Several voices called out, "A mouse."

"No," said our guide. "Something even smaller than that."

We thought for a while then shrugged our shoulders. He smiled at us and said, "An ant."

He then went on to tell us that an ant can crawl up the elephants trunk, into its brain and send it mad. To avoid this, the elephant sleeps with its trunk in its mouth.

I was buzzing as I went back to my room. I quickly found my diary and wrote down everything he'd said. I finished off by writing, "What a great analogy! There's a message in this!"

Think about it

* Ask the children what they think the message/analogy might be. (It's not just the 'big' sins that can destroy us. Sometimes the 'small' sins are just as destructive.)

The Gift of Values

- *Song of Solomon* talks about the 'little foxes that spoil the vines.' S.O.S 2:15

- What are some small sins that can seem harmless? Get the children to list as many as they can. (White lies? Cheating? Evading taxes?)

- What can we learn from the elephant sleeping with its trunk in its mouth? (We must guard against sin, and take necessary precautions.)

- What are some things a gardener has to be diligent about? (Pulling weeds; protecting plants from frost; killing slugs and aphids.)

- Discuss the following poem:

    > *Sow a thought, reap an action.*
    > *Sow an action, reap a habit.*
    > *Sow a habit, reap a character.*
    > *Sow a character, reap a destiny.*

- Discuss what happens at a testing station for cars. The mechanics are looking not just for huge faults within your vehicle but also small things that will grow to become a problem.

- Discuss the proverb, "A stitch in time saves nine."

Boom clip

When Jacob had just learnt to walk, he loved to play with a wooden sword that Josiah had made. He would toddle up to one of his siblings, point the sword and say, "En garde!" (The children had recently watched a cartoon of The Three Musketeers and the phrase had stuck.) Everyone would laugh at this tiny little thing challenging his brothers and sisters. Sometime later I read a book by Vicki Brady called *Quiet Moments for Home School Moms and Dads*. In it she tells how their family has adopted the phrase 'En garde!' as a code, a warning. Whenever they see someone in a position where greed, power, immorality, or some subtle sin is a threat, they say,

'En garde!' That simple phrase helps them get a reality check when they are fighting over a toy, pushing a sibling around, or looking at questionable movies in the video store. What a great idea!

Something to do

- Show the children some large bean seeds. Ask the children what happens when you plant them. (They grow into plants which eventually have beans.)

- Now put a tiny mustard seed in each of their hands. What would happen if you plant this? (Same answer - it too will grow. It doesn't matter how small a seed is; inherent in it is the power for it to grow and multiply.)

- Have fun with a diamante poem. Diamante poems are specially formatted poems, with seven lines, in the shape of a diamond. They use nouns, adjectives, and gerunds ('ing' words) to describe two opposing topics. The first word and bottom word are opposite nouns.

Follow this pattern:

1. Write a noun in the first line and its opposite noun in the last line.
2. On line two, write two adjectives describing the first noun.
3. On line three write three gerunds relating to the noun.
4. On line four write four words - two related to the noun in line one and two related to the noun in line seven. This is where the crossover happens.
5. On line five write three gerunds relating to the bottom noun.
6. On line six choose two adjectives describing the last noun.
7. And of course on the last line you have the antonym of the noun in line one.
8. For example: what is the opposite of truth? (Lies, deception, deceit.) Just writing the poem can help children see a progression.

The Gift of Values

Boom clip

Josiah wrote a diamante poem some time ago, called 'Compromise'.

truth
pure, precious,
guiding, helping, freeing,
honesty, integrity, compromise, deceit,
entangling, hurting, destroying,
dangerous, white
lies

So said...

- "A train is said to have been stopped on one of the United States' railways by flies in the grease-boxes of the carriage wheels. The analogy is perfect. A man in all other respects fitted to be useful, may by some small defect be exceedingly hindered, or even rendered utterly useless." *Charles Spurgeon*

- "It only takes a small nail to bring the most expensive car to a halt." *R J Boom*

- "Watch yourself at all times, and correct yourself before you correct your friends." *Thomas à Kempis*

Words to live by

- "Watch over your heart with all diligence for from it flow the issues of life." *Proverbs 4:23 NASB*

- "Therefore, brethren, be all the more diligent to make certain about His calling and choosing you; for as long as you practise these things, you will never stumble." *2 Peter 1:10 NIV*

- "Be devoted to one another in brotherly love; give preference to one another in honour; not lagging behind in diligence, fervent in spirit, serving the Lord." *Romans 12:10, 11 NIV*

- "Sow for yourselves righteousness, reap the fruit of unfailing love, and break up your unploughed ground; for it is time to seek the Lord, until he comes and showers righteousness on you. But you have planted wickedness, you have reaped evil, and you have eaten the fruit of deception." *Hosea 10:12, 13 NIV*

Dig deeper

- Read the book *Gifted Hands*. It is the story of an inner city kid with poor grades and little motivation, who at the age of thirty-three, became director of paediatric neurosurgery at John Hopkins University Hospital. How does the change occur? Incrementally. Ben Carson's mother decides to make her two boys read two books a week. (Prior to this Ben had never read an entire book in his life.) At first it's the hardest thing in the world for him to do. Then comes the amazing day when the teacher asks the class what obsidian is. Ben waits for the others to put up their hands. Then the truth begins to dawn on him. No one else knows! Slowly he raises his hand.

- Read Dr White's story *Perembi and the Leopard*. Perembi kills a leopard and then discovers she had a cub. He can't bear to kill the cub - it looks so cute. He takes it back to the village, and gives it to the children as a pet, despite the chief's warnings. Of course, the leopard grows and grows, until one day it tastes blood, and becomes savage. Finally, it kills Perembi before the chief manages to kill it. The catch phrase of the story is, '*Little leopards become big leopards, and big leopards kill.*' No matter how small the sin, it has within it the seed of death. (You can find this on line at *www.sarahministry.org*. Or you can simply type *Perembi and the Leopard* into your search engine.)

A Pocket of Beans

idget, fidget, fidget. They just couldn't sit still. I looked at my six children in despair. "Listen!" I said for the umpteenth time. There was a moment of silence and then the wriggling began again.

I felt like putting the Bible down, going to my room and shutting the door. Just then an idea came to me. Without even thinking it through properly, I got up and made for the door. "Wait here," I said.

I went out to the garage and returned with a handful of bean seeds. "Hold out your hands," I said. Carefully I placed one fat bean seed in each palm. They looked at me with puzzled looks. I had their attention.

"O.K," I said. "Each of you has the same seed in your hands. Now, I want you all to come outside."

They followed me outside, each clutching their seed.

"Okay, Jake. I want you to run and find Mummy's little trowel." Off he sprinted and returned with the garden trowel. "Now I want you to dig a little hole in our driveway and plant your seed."

We all watched as my five-year-old dug a hole in the gravel, placed his seed in it, and covered it up again.

Then we went to the gate leading into the orchard. "O.K. Milly," I said. "I want you to toss your seed into the orchard area."

She threw it in with gusto, and even before it had hit the ground, six of her chickens had come running. One swift peck and it had disappeared. Now, I hadn't planned that, but I was very grateful to God for helping me out with the illustration!

Then we went out to the roadside, and Eliza planted hers amongst the long grass.

Last of all, we headed to the vegetable garden. Here I got the remaining three children to plant their seeds in the rich black soil.

Jacob watched Sam planting his seed, and then said, "Mum, my seed won't grow very well in the driveway."

I smiled at him and said, "Never mind, Jake. Come inside and we'll talk about it."

As I read the parable of the sower and the seeds, they were all very switched on! And when I told them that every single morning when we have devotions, they each receive a seed, they knew exactly what I meant.

What followed then was a great discussion about planting seeds, weeding and tending a garden - the garden of our hearts.

Think about it

- ❖ Read together Matthew 13:3-8. What does the soil represent? (Our hearts.)

- ❖ We are all responsible for the soil in the garden of our hearts. Is it good soil? Is it hard? Are there weeds? Ask your children what sort of soil do they think is in their hearts. Explain that they can choose what type of soil the word of God is planted into in their hearts. In fact, they are the *only* ones who can choose the type of soil their garden will have.

- ❖ Every time we hear the Bible being read, we are given some seeds. What do we do with them? Where do we plant them? Will they grow?

Something to do

- ❖ Do some gardening together. Till the soil and plant some seeds. (If the above activity had been planned rather than spontaneous, I would have used sunflower seeds instead of beans, given that none of my children are that keen on beans!)

- ❖ As your children nurture their garden, it will be an ongoing lesson of how important it is to tend to our gardens/hearts.

The Gift of Values

- ❖ A fun activity for young children is to make a seed man. Cut a short length of pantyhose and tie a knot in one end. Fill it with potting mix and then sprinkle some grass seed in the middle on top of the mix. Tie a knot in the other end. The two knots will be the man's ears. Let your child draw a face on the man with a felt pen, and then put him in a saucer on the window sill. Make sure they remember to water him, and he will soon sport a lovely crop of long green hair. They last for ages, and the children will have a lot of fun giving their man all types of radical haircuts.

- ❖ Teach your children of appropriate age how to light the fire. Just the other night, Chris was teaching one of the younger children. She did very well at getting it going, but forgot to look after it. Alas, within a very short time there was nothing but a few smouldering ashes. It's a good lesson in diligence. We don't just light a fire, we must also *tend* the fire. It's not how we start something, but how we finish.

So said...

- ❖ "Brethren, tend to the fire. Tend to the fire, for it is the nature of a fire to go out." *William Booth on his deathbed*

- ❖ "I never could have done what I have done without the habits of punctuality, order, and diligence, without the determination to concentrate myself on one subject at a time." *Charles Dickens*

- ❖ "Enthusiasm is what fires us out of the starting blocks. Diligence is what carries us through the middle miles and over the finish line." *R J Boom*

Words to live by

- "Watch over your heart with all diligence, for from it flow the springs of life." *Proverbs 4:23 NASB*

- "I went past the field of the sluggard, past the vineyard of the man who lacks judgment; thorns had come up everywhere, the ground was covered with weeds, and the stone wall was in ruins. I applied my heart and learned a lesson from what I saw: A little sleep, a little slumber, a little folding of the hands to rest - and poverty will come on you like a bandit and scarcity like an armed man." *Proverbs 24:30-34 NIV*

Dig deeper

- Read *Granny Brand* by Dorothy Clarke Wilson. It's a wonderful story of a young girl who hears the call to India. At her church farewell she chose as her text *1 Kings 20:11:* "Let not him who girds on his amour boast as him who takes it off." In other words, wait until after the fight to boast! It's how you finish that counts. Evelyn Brand needed plenty of diligence in preparing for her language exams. She found language learning extremely difficult and almost despaired of ever passing. But by studying hard, she just managed to scrape through. And what a lifetime of love and service she gave to India!

ଔ

The Gift of Values

The Ants and the Grasshopper
by Aesop

One fine day in winter some ants were busy drying their store of corn, which had got rather damp during a long spell of rain. Presently up came a grasshopper and begged them to spare her a few grains. "For," she said, "I'm simply starving."

The ants stopped work for a moment, though this was against their principles. "May we ask," said they, "what you were doing with yourself all last summer? Why didn't you collect a store of food for the winter?"

"The fact is," replied the grasshopper, "I was so busy singing that I hadn't the time."

"If you spent the summer singing," replied the ants, "you can't do better than spend the winter dancing." And they chuckled and went on with their work.

Boom clip

One of our favourite family games is a fast version of Scrabble. One evening I was playing this with the family, and Jess, my six- year-old niece, was my team mate. She had the job of watching the letters that were turned over in the centre of the table and calling out if she saw a two letter word. As the game progressed she got louder and louder. "It! He! Us! Me! No!!!!" And so it went on. But the all-time favourite word which I taught her that night was 'Ai.' According to the dictionary an ai is a three-toed South American sloth. That word won us a lot of points over the night as Jess yelled out "Ai!" whenever an 'a' and an 'i' appeared in the middle.

Later that night, Jess was fast asleep in our room on a mattress on the floor. Suddenly, she sat bolt upright in bed, shouted out, "Ai!" then fell back on her pillow fast asleep.

Diligence

Sloths are amazing creatures. The word 'sloth' comes from a Hebrew word meaning 'idle'. And they are! Sloths sleep at least fifteen hours a day. A sloth can stay in a single tree all its life, and will die of starvation if food is not easily accessible. Moths and algae take advantage of this lazy animal, and a sloth can have a bad musty smell from all the algae!

This is where we get the word 'slothful' from, meaning 'lazy, and unwilling to work.'

Laziness is defined as 'inactivity resulting from a dislike of work.' Now here, parents, lies a challenge and a half! Can we possibly teach our children to *like* work?

"I don't think it's possible," says Josiah, who has just come into the office and read the question! Then he adds, "But with God, anything is possible!"

Exactly! And if we make sure we offer positive role models, we'll be a long way already down this bumpy, difficult road. But if we moan and grumble as we fix dinner, do the ironing, or clean the house, it's not looking good! One of our important challenges is to try and make chore time as pleasant as possible. Be positive as you work together. And when the house is spic and span, even if it only stays that way for a few short, delicious moments, make sure you celebrate it with the children. Let them feel the satisfaction that comes from the achievement.

Happiness, as Aristotle once said, resides in activity, both physical and mental. It is a great mistake if we equate enjoyment with amusement or relaxation or mere entertainment. Life's greatest joys are not found in what we do *apart from* the work in our lives, but rather *with* the work of our lives. As parents we know this to be true! Children are hard work! But is there any greater joy?

The Gift of Values

Think about it

- Why hadn't the grasshopper prepared for the winter?

- What did the ants tell her to do?

- How do ants compare with sloths? In what ways are they different in their habits? Read Proverbs 6:6. (Ants don't need a leader telling them what to do. They are busy and productive.)

- Ask your children if they think they are more like an ant or a sloth! When I asked my children this, the two little boys both declared themselves to be ants. Milly was perhaps a little more honest or realistic! She thought for a few seconds, then said, "I think I'm half ant, half sloth."

- Why did Nick Willis win a gold medal at the 2006 Olympics? Why did any of the athletes win a medal? (They were diligent in their training. They put in the long hours. They valued the chance to compete with the best, and therefore were willing to forgo late nights and all kinds of foods; they were willing to get up early in the morning while everyone else was still asleep, and do the hard miles. You will never find a lazy athlete at the Olympics!)

Diligence

Something to do

- Get each child to choose a famous athlete. You can search for ideas at the library or do a Google search for Olympic athletes. You'll have to help the little ones do this, but even they will enjoy reporting back to the family everything they can remember about the athlete and their sport. Once they've done this, ask them what they think each athlete has in common. (Commitment to training/discipline/diligence.)

- "Go to the ant." *Proverbs 6:6-8 NIV* What an amazing example of industry and diligence an ant is! Do some research on ants, then go outside and watch them for a while. Put out some large crumbs and watch the ants drag them away.

- Get the children to copy a picture of a sloth in a tree.

- Here's a suggestion for the bold among you. Buy your children a pet. There is nothing like having the responsibility of caring for an animal to teach our children diligence. The benefits will be worth every sleepless night caused by a lonely, whining puppy; every little 'mess' your child has to pick up off the carpet; and every time you have to remind them to feed the chickens.

- Encourage your children to play a sport or learn a musical instrument. Both teach diligence and perseverance.

So said...

- "A man who gives his children habits of industry provides for them better than by giving them a fortune." *Richard Whately*

- "If you should put even a little on a little and should do this often, soon this would become big." *Hesiod*

- "The person who removes a mountain begins by carrying away small stones." *Anon*

- "Chop your own wood and it will warm you twice." *Henry Ford*

- "Men who have attained things worth having in this world have worked while others idled, have persevered when others gave up in despair, have practised early in life the valuable habits of self-denial, industry, and singleness of purpose." *Grenville Kleiser*

- "Diligence is the mother of good fortune, and idleness, its opposite, never brought a man to the goal of any of his best wishes." *Miguel De Cervantes*

- "Few things are impossible to diligence and skill. Great works are performed not by strength, but perseverance." *Samuel Johnson*

- "He who labours diligently need never despair; for all things are accomplished by diligence and labour." *Menander of Athens*

- "What we hope ever to do with ease, we must learn first to do with diligence." *Samuel Johnson*

- "In fair weather, mend your sails." *Samuel Rutherford*

Diligence

Words to live by

Indolence and slothfulness are listed as antonyms for diligence. Both are used in the Bible many times.

- "A slothful man does not roast (catch) his prey, but the precious possession of a man is diligence." *Proverbs 12:27 NASB*

- "Poor is he who works with a negligent hand, but the hand of the diligent makes rich." *Proverbs 10:4 NIV*

- "The soul of the sluggard craves and gets nothing, but the soul of the diligent is made fat." *Proverbs 13:4 NIV*

- "Be diligent to present yourself approved to God as a workman who does not need to be ashamed, handling accurately the word of truth." *Proverbs 13:4 NIV*

Dig deeper

- *The Little Red Hen* is a wonderful story about diligence and its rewards, and the laziness that leaves you hungry.

- Watch the video *Wind Dancer* with your younger children. A young girl is paralyzed in a riding accident and part of her healing comes as she is given the responsibility of caring for a horse.

- Read *My Friend Flicka* by Mary O'Hara. A wonderful story about a young boy on a horse ranch. His father reluctantly allows his son to have his own horse, hoping it will teach him some responsibility. He chooses a filly that his dad thinks is 'loco'.

The Gift of Values

- ❖ Read *The Yearling* by Marjorie Rawlings. For Jody, growing up in the backwoods of Florida in the early 1900's, school is the forest, land and river, and lessons are in farming, fishing and hunting. Then one day he discovers a young fawn and takes it home and cares for it.

- ❖ Read *The Poky Little Puppy's Special Day* (a Golden Book for young children). It tells of how the puppy diligently trains for the big race, while other animals are lazing, dancing, eating - anything but training.

- ❖ Read *Piggybook* by Anthony Browne with your young children. It's a fun story about a family who learn to appreciate all the hard work their mother does, and how to help with the work themselves.

Value Five

PERSEVERANCE

Another value of huge importance is perseverance. The dictionary defines perseverance as the ability "to work slowly and steadily" (Collins); "the quality of continuing to try to achieve a particular aim in spite of difficulties" (Oxford).

Perseverance could be described as the ability to carry on, past the point where whatever you are doing is easy, fun, or exciting. Again, this is not an easy thing to master! But the real riches in life are only discovered with perseverance. Without it, our lives are filled with the cheap things - the things that come easily and that don't require hard work. One thing is certain. Our lives *will* hold difficulties and challenges. Our Christian walk is described as a race that we are to run with perseverance *(Hebrews 12:1)*.

We start learning perseverance when we try to take our first stumbling steps as infants. And we will still need it at the very end of our lives, and every day prior to that. One of the quotes in this section talks about patience, persistence and perspiration. I think if you wrap those three up together, you have the genetic make-up of perseverance.

The history books are full of inspiring tales of how people have persevered through difficulties and trials, and gone on to achieve great things. It goes without saying that if they had not shown perseverance, the history books would have had no cause to mention them.

☙

The Gift of Values

"I Can Plod"

William Carey, the great missionary to India, was asked once, "To what do you owe your incredible success?" He thought for a couple of seconds, then replied, "I can plod. I can persevere in any given pursuit. To this I owe everything."

When years of Carey's translation work were destroyed by fire in 1812, he was devastated. He wrote home to England, 'Our printing office was totally destroyed by fire. This is a heavy blow, as it will stop our printing the Scriptures for a long time. I wish to be still and know that the Lord, He is God, and to bow to His will in everything. He will no doubt bring good out of this evil, but at present the providence is very dark."

Despite the huge loss, Carey resolved to begin again, and determined in his heart that this time he would do an even better job.

Carey was right about God's goodness. The news of the fire prompted huge gifts from England and gave his work in India more publicity than ever before. By the end of two months, $50,000 had been raised. Within three months, the presses were running faster than ever before, and by the end of the year all the lost typefaces had been recast. And Carey himself produced translation work that was greatly improved over the manuscripts that had been lost in the fire.

I'm going to coin a new word in honor of William Carey. Plodability - the ability to stick at something even when the going gets really hard and slow, and you don't seem to be making a lot of progress.

We have a similar example of perseverance in our own New Zealand history.

Robert Maunsell, Missionary Pioneer

Robert Maunsell left Ireland in 1835 and arrived in Paihia, New Zealand, on December 21, 1835. After three years on Mokatoa Island in the Manukau Harbour, he moved to Maraetai. Within a year his church congregation had grown to two hundred and fifty, and a school was also prospering. He wrote in his diary about the Maori people, "The desire for knowledge, I may say with truth, amounts to a great thirst. If I could afford the time, they would occupy most of my days in answering their questions and giving instruction. Not only have they excellent memories, but they are very communicative of their knowledge."

By 1840, Robert wrote, "Of the 7000 natives in our district, we compute that fully three-fourths have embraced the Gospel."

Three years later, however, tragedy struck. Within a very short space of time, three fires destroyed most of Robert and Susan's possessions. All Robert's books, and years of his translation work went up in smoke.

However, like William Carey, he resolved to start again from scratch. To begin again can be so daunting. But start again he did, and in 1857 his great work was completed, and his translation of the Old Testament was printed and in the hands of the Maori people.

Think about it

❖ Ask the children if they can think of anyone in the Bible who showed great perseverance. Noah, building the ark *(Genesis 6:12)*. He worked for a hundred and twenty years before the rain came!

❖ Ask your children, "Have you ever spent ages doing something or making something, and then had it destroyed? Perhaps someone knocked down your amazing LEGO creation. What was your reaction? Were you willing to start all over again?"

The Gift of Values

Something to do

- Find a photo of the great Egyptian pyramids. Tell the children that an Arabian proverb talks of two things that can scale the mighty pyramids. Ask the children for ideas of what those two things could be.

- "There are two things that can scale the mighty pyramids - the eagle and the snail." *Arabian Proverb*

- The eagle - can any of the children think of a verse about eagles? *(Isaiah 40:28-31.)* We are to rise (soar) with wings like eagles. Explore an encyclopaedia or the internet for interesting information about eagles.

- The snail - ask the children what they think about snails. (They are slow, but persistent.) Sometimes it's easy to soar above the obstacles, to rise above the difficulties. But at other times, we need to be like the snail. Slow and steady. Plod, plod, plod.

- Get the children to draw an eagle and a snail in their books.

- The young ones might like to go and find a snail each and have some snail races!

Boom clip

While writing this chapter on my computer, the electricity went off in the storm. When I realised that I hadn't saved my work, I groaned. Then I saw the irony of it. Here I was writing about two men who had lost years of translation work in fires, and I was groaning about one chapter! Ah, I've got a lot to learn.

So said...

- "Never, never, never give up!" *Winston Churchill* (Ink it. Try writing each of the 'nevers' in a different style or in calligraphy.)

- "We can do anything we want to do if we stick to it long enough." *Helen Keller*

Perseverance

- "How many a man has thrown up his hands at a time when a little more effort, a little more patience would have achieved success?" *Elbert Hubbard*

- "It's not that I'm so smart, it's just that I stay with problems longer." *Albert Einstein*

- "What this power is, I cannot say. All I know is that it exists and it becomes available only when you are in that state of mind in which you know exactly what you want and are fully determined not to quit until you get it." *Alexander Graham Bell*

- "It's the plugging away that will win you the day. So don't be a piker old pard! Just draw on your grit; it's so easy to quit. It's the keeping your chin up that's hard." *Robert W Service*

If you think you are beaten, you are;
If you think that you dare not, you don't;
If you'd like to win and you think you can't
It's almost certain that you won't.

If you think you'll lose, you've lost;
For out in the world you'll find
Success begins with a fellow's will -
It's all in the state of mind.

If you think that you are out-classed, you are;
You've got to think high to rise;
You've got to be sure of yourself before
You can ever win a prize.

Life's battles don't always go
To the stronger or faster man;
But sooner or later, the man who wins
Is the man who thinks he can.
– Author unknown

Words to live by

- "Blessed is the man who perseveres under trial; for once he has been approved, he will receive the crown of life, which the Lord has promised to those who love Him." *James 1:12 NIV*

- "So do not throw away your confidence; it will be richly rewarded. You need to persevere so that when you have done the will of God, you will receive what he has promised." *Hebrews 10:35-36 NIV*

- "We also rejoice in our sufferings, because we know that suffering produces perseverance; perseverance, character; and character, hope." *Romans 5:3-4 NIV* (N.B Take the time to discuss this with your children. Suffering produces perseverance. Not what we like to hear, but oh, so true.)

Dig deeper

- Read *The Tortoise and the Hare* to the younger children.

- Read *The Little Hero of Holland*. It tells the story of a young boy who sees a tiny hole breaking through in the huge dykes. He puts his finger in it and stays there all night, waiting for someone to come and help. He knows that if he lets go, the hole will get bigger and bigger until the dam bursts and the villages are flooded.

- Read about the Little Steam Engine who tries to get up the steep hill. ("I think I can, I know I can!")

- Watch the video *Wild Hearts Can't Be Broken*. It's the inspiring true story of a young girl who dives horses from a high tower at the circus. Then one day, the horse gets a fright just before the dive. They fall awkwardly and Senora has her eyes open when they hit the water. She doesn't realise it, but her retinas are detached, and very shortly she is blind. It is a wonderful story of courage and perseverance as she learns to ride and dive again.

Perseverance

- ❖ Read the full story of Carey's 40 years in India in the book, *William Carey. The Shoemaker Who Pioneered Modern Missions,* by Ben Alex.
- ❖ Study the life and achievements of Thomas Edison.
- ❖ *The Lord of the Rings* is a classic story of courage, friendship and perseverance.
- ❖ Read about Joni Erickson Tada, and her struggle as she learns to cope with disability. She is a wonderful example of the perseverance that is produced by suffering.
- ❖ Do a project on the life and achievements of New Zealander, Mark Inglis. You could read his autobiography, and also his book, *Off the Front Foot.* Mark lost both his legs after being trapped in an ice cave on Mount Cook for two weeks. Since then, he has won silver at the Paralympics for cycling, and successfully climbed Mount Cook with metal legs. Just tonight we heard the amazing news on television that Mark has succeeded in reaching the summit of Mount Everest. What an incredible example of perseverance!
- ❖ Memorize together the poem, *Try, Try Again*:

> *'Tis a lesson you should heed.*
> *Try, try again;*
> *If at first you don't succeed,*
> *Try, try again;*
>
> *Then your courage should appear,*
> *For if you will persevere,*
> *You will conquer, never fear;*
> *Try, try again.*

The Gift of Values

Boom clip

We first came across this poem in the book *Caddie Woodlawn*. Caddie's young brother, Warren, had to recite a portion of the poem in front of the whole school. He practised for days, and became more and more worked up about it. Finally the big day arrives and he is called up on stage. He takes a deep breath and then says in a loud voice, "If at first you don't fricassee, fry, fry a hen!"

We laughed about that for days, and the children would call it out every time Jacob got muddled up trying to recite Psalm 119:9-10. "How can a young man keep his way pure? By living according to Your word. I seek You with all my heart. Do not let me stray from Your commands. I have hidden Your word in my heart so I not might… so I… so I not might… so I MIGHT NOT sin against You!"

Just today I was making a Zorro cloak for Samuel. Everything was going wrong. The thread kept breaking and I couldn't get the tension right. Grrr. Then Sam came to see how I was getting on. I told him that everything was going wrong. He patted my arm and said, "If at first you don't succeed, fry, fry a hen, eh Mum?" It was a timely word for me! I persisted and soon he was running through the house, black cape flying behind him. He looked fantastic. Now for Jacob's one!

"You're Just Not Suited!"

Adapted from the story *Not Good Enough* by Dave and Neta Jackson

Gladys shuffled uneasily on her chair and made herself look the principal in the eyes. A thousand thoughts streamed through her mind. *What is he going to say? What if he tells me they don't want me to stay? I must go to China!*

"I'm sorry, Gladys," said the principal gently, "your grades for the first quarter are… well, very poor. We feel it would be a waste of your time, effort and money to continue."

Gladys looked at him with stricken eyes. "But sir, all my life I have felt God has called me to China."

The principal of the China Inland Mission training school looked at her and shook his head. "By the time you finished here you would be nearly thirty. That is far too old to learn a difficult language like Chinese. I'm sorry Gladys, but there is no longer a place for you here. We feel you are just not suited for missionary work."

He looked at her with compassion and added gently, "I am however able to find you a job as a housekeeper."

A housekeeper! Gladys walked from the room with a heavy heart.

However, the two retired missionaries who hired her as their housekeeper encouraged Gladys in her interest in missions. They found her a job as a Rescue Sister in South Wales, patrolling the streets for runaway girls - girls who all too often fell into the hands of criminals down on the docks. However, a bad case of pneumonia sent Gladys home to her mother in London. It was there that she heard of an elderly missionary in China, Jennie Lawson, who needed someone to help her.

"That's me!" said Gladys to herself. "I will go and help her."

As soon as she recovered, Gladys got a job as a maid. She began to save every penny to pay her way to China.

The Gift of Values

The door bell chimed as Gladys entered the travel agency. "How much does it cost to travel to China?" she asked the travel agent.

The man smiled at the tiny woman in front of him, dressed in a thin shabby coat. She was obviously poor.

"Ninety pounds, if you go by boat," he said.

Ninety pounds! Gladys felt the two pounds in her pocket. "Is there a cheaper way?" she asked.

The travel agent shrugged. 'If you go by train it will cost forty-five, but...."

"I'll take it!" cried Gladys. "Please write me a ticket. I will come in every Friday with more money until it is paid off."

"I'm sorry," said the man. "Russia and China are at war. The border is closed. You can't go by train right now."

Gladys beamed at him. "By the time I have saved enough money, the war will be over," she said confidently.

Two years later, on October 15, 1930, Gladys said goodbye to her parents and began the long trip to China. She looked more like a gypsy than a missionary, with her orange frock worn over her coat, and a bag clanging with pots and pans and a kettle. She carried two suitcases, one stocked with food.

Four weeks and five thousand miles later, the determined five foot woman, who had been told she would never make the grade, stood in front of a run-down inn in the mountain town of Yangcheng. She was ready to begin what she had always known she was called to do. The long road she had travelled to reach that goal was called 'Perseverance'.

Think about it

- How easy do you think it would have been for Gladys to give up?
- Why was she so determined to go?
- Did she demonstrate plodability?
- Do you find it easy to finish a task, or are you in the habit of stopping halfway through?
- Can you develop and cultivate plodability? How?

Something to do

- Each choose a task that will take some perseverance to see it through. It might be cleaning under your bed, or cleaning out your wardrobe. (I've just thought of a great one for Milly - cleaning out her chicken coop!) Design a special 'Gladys Aylward Award' and present it to those who stuck with the job and finished it. (I should have won this for my Zorro cloaks!)
- Get each of your children to choose something they are going to save up for. Encourage them over the next few days or weeks to stay true to their goal. Make sure they get a 'Gladys Aylward Award' at the end!

So said...

- "Don't bother about genius. Don't worry about being clever. Trust to hard work, perseverance and determination. And the best motto for a long march is, "Don't grumble. Plug on!" *Sir Frederick Treves*
- "Patience, persistence and perspiration make an unbeatable combination for success." *Napoleon Hill*
- "Genius is 1% inspiration and 99% perspiration." *Thomas Edison*

Words to live by

- "By faith he left Egypt, not fearing the King's anger; he persevered because he saw him who is invisible." *Hebrews 11:27 NIV*. N.B Moses had an even longer journey than Gladys! He needed a lot of perseverance as he tried to cope with a large contingent of grumblers.

- "Therefore since we are surrounded by such a great cloud of witnesses, let us throw off everything that hinders and the sin that so easily entangles, and let us run with perseverance the race marked out for us." *Hebrews 12:1 NIV*

Dig deeper

- Read more about Gladys Aylward in *The Small Woman* by Alan Burgess.

- If you haven't already done so, watch the movie *The Inn of the Six Happinesses.*

- Watch the DVD *The Prince of Egypt* with your younger children.

Wheelbarrow Jack
Adapted from a true story by Jane Thomson

Gold! Everyone was talking about the gold to be discovered at Hyde. Men put their gear and their dreams into packs and set off for Hyde.

Jack couldn't afford a pack. But he did own a wheelbarrow. He put his pick and shovel and tin dish into the wheelbarrow, threw in a few clothes and blankets, and set off. He pushed his wheelbarrow for one hundred kilometres until he finally reached the small township of Hyde.

The best spots for digging had already been claimed by then, but he found the side of a hill where no one was working and began.

Day after day, week after week, Jack dug for gold but found nothing.

"You're crazy," said the other miners.

"It's worth a try," replied Jack and just kept on digging.

Then his food ran out. "Can you let me have some food?" he asked the storekeeper. "I'll pay you back as soon as I strike gold."

"Don't reckon you'll ever find gold," said the storekeeper. But he liked Jack. So he gave him some bacon and flour and recorded in a book how much money Jack owed him.

Thanking him, Jack threw the provisions in his wheelbarrow, made his way back to the hill and kept digging.

Day after day it was the same. "Go for it, Wheelbarrow Jack!" laughed the men. But Jack would just smile and wipe away the sweat and keep digging.

One Saturday, Jack made the trip to the store to get some more food.

"I'm sorry, Jack," said the storekeeper. "This is the last food I can give you until you pay me what you owe. Have some sense, man. Give up. Go and find a job in Dunedin and send me the money from there. You're never going to strike gold."

"Don't you worry," said Jack. "I'll pay you back everything I owe."

He returned to his tunnel and kept digging.

The Gift of Values

Two days later, Wheelbarrow Jack struck gold. There was more gold in that hill than had ever been found at Hyde before.

With the first day's gold, he went to the store and paid back the astonished storekeeper. Then he kept on digging. Within a few days, he had found two thousand pounds' worth of gold. That was more money than he could have made if he'd spent the rest of his life working at a job in Dunedin.

And do you think the other miners were still laughing at Wheelbarrow Jack? Not on your life!

Think about it

❖ Can you think of someone in the Bible who worked at something for a long time while people laughed at him? (Noah, Nehemiah.)

❖ What are some other valuable things that aren't gold, but still need to be sought after and pursued with perseverance? (Wisdom – *Proverbs 8:19;* God – *Job 22:25;* the proof of our faith – *Peter 1:7;* relationships; truth…)

Something to do

❖ Try memorizing this little verse. Young school children in the early twentieth century learnt it by heart from their McGuffey's reader.

> *The fisher who draws in his net too soon,*
> *Won't have any fish to sell;*
> *The child who shuts up his books too soon,*
> *Won't learn any lessons well.*
> *If you would have your learning stay,*
> *Be patient - don't learn too fast;*
> *The man who travels a mile each day,*
> *May get round the world at last.*

❖ Research about the gold rush in New Zealand. Look up Hyde on the map.

Boom clip

Grrr. I felt like slamming the clay down with my fist and walking away. I stared at the strange shape in front of me and sighed. I had started out that morning with such high hopes. I was going to create a wonderful puppet which we would use at our concerts – a magnificent angel. Instead, I had created a monster – a Neanderthal. So much for Gabriel. Then a little voice piped up beside me. "Keep going, Mum! It's looking great!" I smiled at my little encourager. "Right," I said. And I got some more clay and added some to the sloping forehead of my creation. All afternoon I persevered, and resisted the frequent temptation to smash my work down. And slowly it changed. That evening, I glowed inside as I looked at my puppet – Gabriel! Yep, he was handsome enough! Since that day, I have used the same mould to cast four other puppets – Daniel; the prodigal son, his father, and his older brother. Whenever I see them in a puppet show, I feel so glad I persevered.

Gabriel and Daniel take to the stage
(both made from the same puppet mould).

So said...

- "Patience and fortitude conquer all things." *Ralph Waldo Emerson*

- "How many a man has thrown up his hands at a time when a little more effort, a little more patience, a little more perseverance would have achieved success." *Arnold H. Glasgow*

- "How many people miss opportunity, because it comes dressed in overalls and looks like hard work!" *Thomas Edison*

- "I'd look at one of my stonecutters hammering away at the rock, perhaps a hundred times without as much as a crack showing in it. Yet, at the hundred and first blow it would split in two, and I knew it was not that blow that did it, but all that had gone before." *Jacob A. Riis*

- "Be like a postage stamp. Stick to one thing until you get there." *Josh Billings*

- "Some people plant in the spring and leave in the summer. If you're signed up for a season, see it through. You don't have to stay forever, but at least stay until you see it through." *Jim Rohn*

Words to live by

- ❖ "And let us not lose heart in doing good, for in due time we shall reap if we do not grow weary." *Galatians 6:9 NASB*

- ❖ "Blessed is the man who perseveres under trial; for once he has been approved, he will receive the crown of life, which the Lord has promised to those who love him." *James 1:12 NASB*

The Gift of Values

Dig deeper

- ❖ Read *The Tortoise and The Hare*.
- ❖ Read the story of Helen Keller and Annie Sullivan. Ann refused to give up. And what a treasure the world found in Helen Keller's mind! I recently read that a person told his friend the two great marvels of America were the Grand Canyon and Helen Keller. His friend replied, "I beg to differ. The two marvels of America are Helen Keller and Ann Sullivan."
- ❖ Read *The Story of My Life* by Helen Keller.

Value Six

OBEDIENCE

Having had six children, I've learned one thing about obedience - some children find it easier to obey than others! Some children (and every family needs at least one of these!) seldom even think of disobeying. However, for others, obedience is a daily struggle. I have at least one of both these children. (Perhaps every family needs one of each??) Bedtime for one was a happy affair, with sweet goodnight cuddles after a story and prayers. But for the other child, bedtime was a nightmare - for me at any rate! She just couldn't stay in her bed. She would say goodnight so sweetly and look like a little angel tucked up in her warm bed, but the second I was out the door, she'd be up again. I remember writing in her journal after one particularly difficult night:

"*Another trying bedtime! A story, pray together, sing the lullaby, lights out – seconds later out of bed, opening the door. Warned, tucked back in bed. Up again, playing in Ellie's bed. Put back in own bed. Up again, this time hiding in the tiny cupboard at the bottom of the wardrobe. Tucked back in again. Minutes later, looking out the window, nappies pulled off. Oh, Emily! When will you learn. Growl from Daddy this time. 9.30 pm finally asleep. Yippee! Obedience does not come easily to you, darling, it seems. Daddy and I are doing our best to train you and teach you the importance of obedience. We long with all our hearts that you will grow up to love the Lord with all your heart and obey Him in love.*"

The Gift of Values

Hmmm. I'm sure many of you have had similar struggles. Of course bedtime isn't an issue of life and death, although sometimes it feels like it! But the next entry I had written in Milly's diary was. *"Today I looked up just in time to see you climbing down the ladder into the pool with no swimming tyre on. Just seconds before I had told you not to go near the steps. Scary to think how quickly and quietly a disaster can happen."*

Just a word here. Our strong willed children can seem such a lot of work, while the compliant child is a salve to our frayed nerves. But each different personality has its own challenges. It's just they're a lot more obvious in the strong-willed child, the leader, the 'lion'. They wear their feelings on their sleeves, and *everybody* knows what they're going through! But although obedience might be a difficult lesson to learn for our strong willed child, they probably excel in courage!

On the other hand, our quiet, reserved children might not struggle with obedience, but they might find honesty more difficult. We need to celebrate our children's differences, and consistently guide and encourage them in their weak areas.

Our children need to know that both obedience and disobedience have consequences. Some of them may be physical, some spiritual. The first death occurred because of disobedience. Death entered the spirit and soul of man with just one bite of the forbidden fruit. So too, our seemingly small disobediences will cause a slow death in our spirits. Obedience is imperative. And as I tell my children, if they can't learn to obey us, their parents, there's no way they will learn to obey God.

The hardest challenge for us as parents is to cultivate in our children a *heart* obedience, not merely outward conformity to the rules. We probably all know the story of the child who was made to sit down. She did sit, but not without saying, "I'm still standing up on the inside!"

One of the most important applications of obedience is learning to listen for God's voice and doing what He says. This is an exciting adventure, full of hidden joys, and one that we need to introduce our children to.

One last thought. True obedience comes from the heart. It is not accompanied by a sour look and angry mutterings. It is an act of love. It brings life and joy. Dear Lord, help us to teach our children this heart obedience!

Boom clip

Samuel sat next to me in the picture theatre and his excitement was tangible. I was a bit worried that he might be scared in the movie, and that wasn't helped when the trailers featured clips of *King Kong*. Sam closed his eyes, and covered his ears. Soon enough, *The Lion, the Witch and the Wardrobe* began. Sam sat riveted in his seat.

We reached the part where the children were shown around the huge house and told in no uncertain terms by the grumpy housekeeper the rules they must obey. "There will be no running, no shouting, no touching of the historical artifacts, and above all, no disturbing of the professor!" I could feel Sam sitting tensely beside me. Then the Pevincy children decide to play hide and seek. Lucy runs through the house looking for somewhere to hide. I didn't think anything of it, but the next minute Sam gripped my arm and whispered urgently in my ear, "No running, eh Mum?!" He was so worried. Then when the children began calling out, he whispered again in an urgent voice, "They shouldn't be shouting!"

Dear Sam! Ever the one to remember the rules and want to obey!

Now, just a word here to those of you who struggle with a strong-willed child. I used to think I was an OK mum until my fourth child, Milly, came along. I used to scoff at the idea of the terrible twos, and then it happened. I didn't know what had struck me. A feisty new element had appeared in the placid Boom family. But how we thank God for our Milly. Our family would be dull and boring without her. She has so much life in her, and she lives life to the full. Everything she does, she does with passion; whether it's running to fling herself into my arms when I pick her up from somewhere, or fiercely fighting for her toy. I remember when she was just little and learning to speak, the cat came inside with a bird in its mouth. Milly was at him in a second, had him by the throat, shook him, and shouted, "SPIT IT OUT!" The astonished cat did as it was told and the bird escaped.

Ah yes, I love my passionate girl. This next Boom clip is especially for those of you who are despairing that you will ever be able to teach your 'Milly' obedience. Don't give up. You will reap a wonderful harvest from your efforts eventually. It's just you're training a champion.

Boom clip

"Well, I'll run away!"

I couldn't help smiling at the feisty little thing that stood in front of me. With curly blonde hair and the bluest of eyes, Milly looked like a little angel. But I don't think angels could ever be as stroppy or strong willed as my six-year-old daughter.

The drama was over school work. The other five children were all keen, teachable students. But not my Milly. She resisted daily and groaned and moaned at everything I told her to do. She was the only one that had ever threatened to run away from home!

"Oh no you won't, Miss Milly," I said with a smile. I bent down and kissed her freckled nose. "You will do your work, and we'll have a good time at school today."

How wrong I was. That day was to be the worst of my home schooling and mothering career. Milly was determined to push me to the limits. She argued, dilly dallied, disobeyed and complained. I can't even remember what it was that finally pushed me over the edge.

"That's it!" I shouted. "That's it! I can't take it any more. You're going to school!" I pushed away from the table and stormed into my room. Milly followed me, wailing.

I sat on my bed, trying to gain control of my frustration and the sense of failure that threatened to swallow me up.

Milly was crying now and pleading with me. "No, Mummy! I'll be good. I promise."

She looked so vulnerable, but something had happened inside my heart. I felt hard and brittle in my defeat.

"I used to love home schooling," I snapped. "But you've ruined it for me!"

Did I say that? How could I have said something so cruel? Milly flinched, and her face crumpled. Immediately I gathered her in my arms and kissed her.

"Oh Milly, I'm so sorry. Mum's just tired, that's all." I stroked her wet face.

But I still felt ghastly. Horrible, dark thoughts began tormenting me. *She can't run away now - she's only six. But she might when she's sixteen.* It was as if I were staring into a future of rebellion and pain. All the hope and optimism I'd had for my precious daughter's life seemed to shrivel up and die.

We sat there holding each other until we had both stopped crying. But I couldn't escape the empty, despairing feeling inside. Eliza, my ten-year-old, came into the room and said in a sweet, caring voice, "I've finished all my school work now, Mummy. Shall I take over teaching Milly for the morning?"

That made me feel worse. I had never felt such a failure.

That night after Chris and I had got them all to bed, I retreated to my room and fell to my knees. "Father," I prayed, "You've got to help me. I'm scared. I've lost hope for my daughter. I can't teach her to obey. All I can see is rebellion and heartache ahead. Please, give me a word, a promise for her life. Something I can hold on to."

I was almost too scared to wake up the next morning. I couldn't bear another day like the one I'd just had. After reading a Psalm and trying to encourage my heart, I went into the office to check my email. There was just one. Four lines from a missionary friend in Asia. I'd written to her that week and told her Milly had fallen on a tree root and broken her collar bone.

"I was so sorry to hear about dear Milly's accident. But it will take more than a broken bone to slow her down! She's a champion!"

She's a champion! The words leapt off the screen and straight into my wounded heart. I put my face in my hands and wept. And as I did, hope filled my heart again. God had spoken to me! He saw my Milly as a champion! I laughed and cried as I spoke the truth out loud again and again.... "She's a champion! Milly's a champion!"

And so, with just four words, the Lord turned despair into hope, my sense of failure into a sense of purpose. I'm training a champion - a little blonde, blue eyed girl with that extra grit, determination and strength that a champion needs.

My Milly's a champion!

Go for it, mums and dads! Enjoy reading this chapter about obedience. Enjoy the challenge of training your champions. And remember, an oak tree doesn't grow overnight.

Milly the champion

"Who, me?!"

George's eyes flashed with excitement behind his dark rimmed glasses as he looked at us. "God will speak to you!"

"Who, me?!" I squeaked. I couldn't help it. It just came out. But by the look of my three friends, I had just said what they were all thinking anyway. We were all brand new Christians. I was sixteen and had given my heart to the Lord three weeks earlier. The best night of my week was when we got together at George's house to learn more about the Lord. George wasn't your average, ordinary Christian. At least not the type I'd met before. Here he was saying that God would speak to me. That I could hear His voice!

He grinned at our nervous, excited faces and said, "Okay guys! Here's your homework. I want you to go home and *ask* God to speak to you. Make sure you listen, and then when you hear His voice, make sure you obey!" He beamed and wriggled his bushy eyebrows. "When we get together again next week, you can all share what happened."

Man! Was this for real? Surely God wouldn't be bothered talking to me? I was pretty sure He wouldn't, but that night before I fell asleep, I did what George had said. I asked.

"Lord, would You speak to me? I really want to hear Your voice."

I woke early the next morning. After reading a few chapters of Luke I started to get ready for school. And then I heard it. It was like a whisper from somewhere inside. A thought. An impression.

I want you to go Marcia's house and tell her that you've become a Christian.

No way. That wasn't God speaking to me. Marcia was a friend that I used to do a lot with. But I hadn't seen her for six months. Don't know where the thought came from, but it couldn't have been from God.

The Gift of Values

There it was again. A gentle whisper. I started feeling really nervous. There was no way I was going to just turn up on an old friend's doorstep and tell her, "Guess what? I've become a Christian!" She'd laugh me out of town.

I tried to ignore it. But it didn't go away. I wriggled and squirmed, but couldn't escape it. Somehow I just knew that God was talking to me and I had heard Him. And George had said that I'd better obey!

I didn't want school to finish that day. I was so nervous. *What will I say? How will I start? Do I just knock on her door and blurt it out?* The questions spun round and round in my head.

I decided to walk the few blocks to her house rather than bike, just to give me a little bit more time. But it was agony. My feet felt as if a ship's anchor was dragging them through the concrete. That made me think about Jonah who had tried to disobey God. Well I wasn't running away yet, but I sure felt like it. In fact I think if it wasn't for George expecting us to 'listen and obey', I would have bolted home.

"Help me Lord! What am I going to say? What if she shuts the door in my…"

Just then I heard my name. "Hey, Rose!"

I spun around and saw a girl biking towards me. I couldn't believe my eyes. It was Marcia's sister, Kate. She pulled up beside me. "Hi, Rose! Whatcha been up to?" She jumped off her bike and started walking beside me. "Marcia was just saying the other day that she'd love to catch up with you."

It was as easy as falling off a bike. I told Kate that three weeks ago I'd become a Christian and that my life had really changed.

"No way!' she said. 'That's so cool! Hey, what are you up to now?"

I shrugged my shoulders. "Nothing much."

"Why don't you come home with me now? You can tell us all about it. Marcia would love to see you."

So I arrived at Marcia's house with my very own escort. Kate threw her bike against the house and yelled out, 'Hey, Marcia! Guess what? Rose is here and she's become a Christian!"

So much for worrying about how to start!

Boy, you should have seen their faces when I got to the part where God had spoken to me and told me to come and talk to them!

"You mean He knows about *me*?" said Marcia. 'He cares about *me*?"

I nodded, grinning.

"But what about this?!" piped in Kate. "He used *me* to help you. Wow! How cool is that!?"

We talked for at least an hour. They were so keen to hear everything I could tell them about God. Both of them were crying when we finally prayed together.

I floated home that afternoon, and all the anchors in the sea couldn't have held me down. God had spoken to me! And I had obeyed! And the amazing thing was, in the end it wasn't that hard after all! All I needed to do was start obeying and He prepared the way.

Roll on next Wednesday night! I couldn't wait to share my exciting discovery. I could hear God's voice!

Think about it

❖ Does God want to speak to us?

❖ How does He speak to us? (An inner voice; through the Word; dreams; visions.)

❖ When He speaks, what must we do? (Obey!)

❖ How can you make sure that it is God speaking to you? (God will never contradict His Word; check it out with other wise people you respect.)

Boom clip

When Josiah and Kate were just five and four respectively, I had just read to them the account of God calling out to Samuel in the night. I was telling them that they would learn to hear God's voice too; that the Lord wanted to talk to them.

"Mummy," said Josiah, "I haven't heard God speak to me yet."

I was just about to tell him not to worry; that he would learn to hear God's voice, when little Kate piped up.

"I have, Mummy! I have!"

I turned to look at her, smiling at her large earnest eyes. "Have you, darling? When?"

"Just the other day, when we were praying." She was so excited about it.

"That's wonderful, Katie," I said. "What did He say?"

Kate looked at me with a big smile on her face.

"He said, 'Hello'!"

Something to do

- ❖ Encourage your children to *listen* for the voice of God. One of the things George asked each of us brand new Christians to do was set aside $5.00 and ask the Lord to show us in the next week who we should give it to. I remember being so excited about it. Would God possibly talk to me? Would He show me who I was to give it to? He did! Part of the exercise was learning to listen, to be alert for both God's gentle nudging and also opportunities that come our way. Try this with your children. It can be any amount of money. They will be so excited when they each report back.

- ❖ Design an 'Obedience Award'. This can be presented to whoever cheerfully and quickly obeys. Emphasis on the cheerfully and quickly!

Obedience

Train yourself to always acknowledge and praise swift and cheerful obedience.

- Read together the story of the two sons in Matthew 21:28-32. One says, "Yes, I will go," and doesn't. The other says, "No, I won't go," but later changes his mind and obeys. Which one did the will of the father?

So said...

- "True obedience is true freedom." *Henry Ward Beecher*
- "The ship that will not obey the helm will have to obey the rocks." *English Proverb*
- "I have thought about it a great deal, and the more I think, the more certain I am that obedience is the gateway through which knowledge, yes, and love too, enter the mind of the child." *Anne Sullivan*
- "Wicked men obey from fear; good men, from love." *Aristotle*
- "Obedience without faith is possible, but not faith without obedience." *Anon*
- "We have to *learn* obedience. It comes no other way. A tedious lesson perhaps, but one that yields inconceivable blessings." *R J Boom*

Words to live by

There are countless verses about obedience in the Bible. And many wonderful stories about people who chose to obey God, even when it was difficult.

- "I delight to do Thy will, O my God; Thy law is within my heart." *Psalm 40:8 NASB*
- "If anyone loves me, he will obey My teaching." *John 14:23 NIV*

The Gift of Values

- ❖ "If you obey My commands, you will remain in My love, just as I have obeyed My Father's commands and remain in His love. I have told you this so that My joy may be in you and that your joy may be complete." *John 15:10, 11 NIV*

- ❖ "Dear friends, if our heart does not condemn us, we have confidence before God and receive from Him anything we ask, because we obey His commands and do what pleases Him. And this is His command: to believe in the name of His Son, Jesus Christ, and to love one another as He commanded us. Those who obey His commands live in Him, and He in them." *1 John 3:2 1-24 NIV*

Dig deeper

- ❖ Read the story of Jonah. This is a great one to act out if you have small children. We use a sheet for the ship, with several of the children holding the corners and tossing it about wildly, while poor Jonah sits inside it and tries not to be thrown overboard. The best part is when the sailors are *allowed* to toss him into the sea!

- ❖ Discuss the fact that our obedience or disobedience usually affects someone else also.

- ❖ Read the story of the Lord calling to Samuel in the night *(1 Samuel 3)*. Explain to your children that we *learn* to hear God's voice.

☙

The Widow's Birthday

My mum has always been a wonderful example to me of listening to the Lord, and obeying, even if she thinks what He's asked her to do seems foolish. On this particular day, Mum bustled around the house, happy to have a day off from teaching. As she vacuumed the lounge, a thought gently came to her.

Ring Patricia at the school and ask her to lunch.

Patricia was the new secretary at the Christian school where Mum taught.

Mum kept vacuuming and tried to push the thought away. Surely it wasn't God speaking to her, because He knew very well that it was her only day off.

Ring Patricia and ask her to lunch.

There it was again. As clear as a bell. Perhaps Patricia was feeling lonely? She had only recently been widowed and emigrated to New Zealand from England. Mum stopped the vacuum cleaner and went to the phone.

Patricia's voice sounded bright and cheerful as she gladly accepted Mum's invitation.

Mum put the phone down, glad to have obeyed, and began to finish the vacuuming. Then the Lord's voice gently spoke again.

Prepare a tray for Patricia with your best china. Make her a bookmark with a verse on it, and put the gift of a handkerchief on the tray. Make her a cup of tea and then let her rest for a while on her own.

Mum obeyed.

When Patricia arrived, Mum gave her a warm hug and took her to the sunroom. She explained that the Lord had spoken to her and prompted her to do all these things.

The Gift of Values

Patricia's eyes filled with tears. "I know why you were given those instructions," she said. "Today is my birthday, and not a soul in New Zealand knows!"

Think about it

- ❖ How do you think Patricia felt after the lunch? (She would have known that the Lord knew all about her and loved her. She would have felt so cherished.)

- ❖ Was it a hard thing the Lord asked Mum to do? (No. Very often He asks us to do simple things, and yet so often we miss the blessings that would have been ours by not heeding His voice.)

- ❖ How open are you to hearing the little whispers in your heart that come from God?

Boom clip

I will never forget the day the Lord spoke to me while we were doing a concert at a church. A young girl was playing the keyboard prior to Chris and I going on stage. She looked about sixteen or maybe seventeen. All of a sudden, a verse came into my mind, and with it the thought that I was to give the verse to this girl. As soon as we had finished singing I looked up the verse. When I saw it, I knew I must have heard wrong.

"Do not be afraid; you will not suffer shame. Do not fear disgrace; you will not be humiliated. You will forget the shame of your youth and remember no more the reproach of your widowhood. For your Maker is your husband - the Lord Almighty is his name - the Holy One of Israel is your redeemer; he is called the God of all the earth. The Lord will call you back as if you were a wife deserted and distressed in spirit - a wife who married young, only to be rejected," says your God. "For a brief moment I abandoned you, but with deep compassion I will bring you back." *Isaiah 54:4-7 NIV*

What a weird verse for a young girl! I must have heard wrong. But the thought persisted and I knew I had to do something. So I did the next best thing. I mentioned it to the pastor's wife. She listened in amazement and then said, "Oh, Rose! You must share that with her! She has just lost her husband in a tree felling accident. They had only been married three months."

I couldn't believe my ears. Married! She looked as if she should be in high school. Why had I doubted? Deep down I had known it was God speaking to me, but it seemed such an odd verse for a young girl like her.

I will never forget the look on her face as I gently shared those precious verses with her. God loved her. He was her husband.

Something to do

- ❖ Each choose a verse of encouragement, and over the next week watch out for someone to share it with. Your children may like to make a bookmark with the verse on that they can give to someone. The whole point again is to learn to listen to the gentle promptings of the Holy Spirit and obey.

So said...

- ❖ "One act of obedience is better than one hundred sermons." *Dietrich Bonhoeffer*
- ❖ "Obedience is the key to every door." *George MacDonald*
- ❖ "I find the doing of the will of God, leaves me no time for disputing about His plans." *George MacDonald* (from his book, *The Marquis of Lossie*)

Words to live by

- "And Samuel said, "Does the Lord delight in burnt offerings and sacrifices as much as in obeying the voice of the Lord? To obey is better than sacrifice, and to heed is better than the fat of rams." *I Samuel 15: 22 NIV* (God wants us to heed - to listen!)

- "The Sovereign Lord has given me an instructed tongue, to know the word that sustains the weary. He wakens me morning by morning, wakens my ear to listen like one being taught. The Sovereign Lord has opened my ears, and I have not been rebellious; I have not drawn back." *Isaiah 50:4-5 NIV*

- "Do not merely listen to the Word, and so deceive yourselves. Do what it says. Anyone who listens to the Word but does not do what it says is like a man who looks at his face in a mirror and, after looking at himself, goes away and immediately forgets what he looks like. But the man who looks intently into the perfect law that gives freedom, and continues to do this, not forgetting what he has heard, but doing it - he will be blessed in what he does." *James 1:22-25 NIV*

- "Everyone should be quick to listen, slow to speak and slow to become angry." *James 1:19 NIV*

Dig deeper

- Read *Is That Really You, God?* by Loren Cunningham. It's a great story of listening and obeying.

- Read about Naaman the leper in 2 Kings 5. He became angry and stormed away when Elijah's servant told him to wash seven times in the dirty Jordan River. His servants reasoned with him and said, "If the prophet had asked you to do some great thing, would you not have done it?"

- Read *Missionary Stories with the Millers* by Mildred A. Martin. It has some exciting stories of people who listened to God's voice and lived lives of obedience.

The Gift of Values

The Knights of the Silver Shield
Adapted from the story by Raymond MacDonald Alden

There was once a magnificent castle with great stone walls and turrets that rose high above a dark forest. Within the forest were many cruel giants. But in the castle was a company of knights, placed there by the king of the land as a protection for travellers who sought to pass through the dangerous forest.

Each of these knights wore a fine suit of armour and carried a long spear. They also possessed a magnificent shield, made of silver, which sometimes shone in the sun with dazzling brightness. The shields had been forged by a great magician long ago. When each young knight received his spurs and armour, a new shield was presented to him. However, the new shield's surface was always dull and cloudy. Its shine only began to appear when the knight fought bravely against the giants, and came to the aid of travellers in need. If the knight proved to be lazy or cowardly, his shield grew duller and duller, until at last the knight became too ashamed to carry it.

If however, that knight fought valiantly and courageously, not only would his shield shine like the morning sun, but a golden star would appear at its very heart. This was the highest honour a knight could receive, and amongst the knights he was spoken of as having 'won his star.'

Now there came a time when all the giants gathered together to do war against the knights. They made camp in a dark hollow not far from the castle, and they were a terrible sight to behold. The windows and doors of the castle were closed and barred, and within its walls the knights prepared themselves for battle. Amongst their company was a young knight, named Sir Roland; a keen and brave fighter he was, and already his shield had begun to shine and bear witness to his brave exploits in the forest. This battle, he thought, would be the great opportunity of his life. Sir Roland hoped he would be placed in the most dangerous position of all, so eager was he to do his duty.

However, it was not to be. The lord of the castle approached him and said, "One brave knight must stay behind and guard the castle's gates. It is you, Sir Roland, whom I have chosen for this."

Sir Roland bit his lip with disappointment. Surely he was not to be denied the honour of fighting with the rest? He struggled to hold his tongue and not argue with his lord.

So it was that when the knights rode out of the castle to face the giants, Sir Roland stayed behind. As the lord of the castle rode by, he instructed the knight again, "Guard the gates until we return, and under no circumstance allow anyone to enter the castle." Then he rode off with his red plume waving above his head, and his spear flashing in the sun.

Sir Roland looked down at the drawbridge and moat. The gate of the castle was high and narrow and could only be reached by a bridge that spanned the moat. The giants had long ago given up trying to attack the castle, so strong were its defences. Sir Roland sighed. It would be a quiet day.

Finally after many hours, Sir Roland saw one of the knights limping towards the gate. His shield was dull.

"I have been hurt," he said, "and cannot fight anymore. But I could watch the gate for you, if you would like to go back in my place."

Sir Roland's heart leaped with joy at these words, but then he remembered his orders.

"I should like very much to go, but a knight belongs where his commander has put him. My place is here at the gate, and I cannot open it even for you. Your place is back at the battle."

At these words the injured knight felt ashamed and presently he turned and went into the forest again.

Another hour passed. Then an old lady appeared asking for food.

"I'm sorry," Sir Roland told her, "but no one is allowed in the castle today. However I shall send you some food, if you will."

As the old woman sat to rest he asked her for news of the battle.

The Gift of Values

"It is a long and difficult battle, I fear," she said. "The giants are fighting fiercely and it goes poorly for the knights. How is it that you are not helping your comrades?"

"Would that I could," answered Sir Roland. "But I have been placed here to guard these gates."

The old lady gave a thin, hard laugh. "One fresh knight would make all the difference. I should think that, since there be no enemies here, you would be much more useful there."

"You may well think so, and so may I," answered Sir Roland. "However neither you nor I are the commander here."

"I suppose," said the old woman then, "that you are the type of knight who likes to avoid the fighting. You are so lucky to have such a good excuse." And she threw him a taunting look.

Sir Roland felt his heart burn within him, and thought that if only she were a man instead of a woman, he would show her whether he liked fighting or not. But he cooled his anger and stayed at his post.

It was not very long before he heard someone calling outside.

"What is it?" he cried. "The castle is closed."

"Are you Sir Roland?" asked an old man in a long black cloak.

"Yes," answered the knight.

"Then you should not be staying here when your commander and the knights are enduring so great a struggle with the giants. See, I have with me a magic sword! This is your chance to be the greatest knight in the kingdom." And with that the little old man drew from under his cloak a magnificent sword that gleamed in the sunlight as if it were covered with diamonds.

"This is the sword of all swords," he said, "and if you will leave your idling here at the castle, and carry it to the battle, none shall stand before you. When you raise it high, the giants shall fall back. Your commander shall be saved, and you shall be crowned the victorious knight - the one who saved the kingdom!"

Now the sword appeared to Sir Roland a truly wonderful sight, and he knew that it was indeed a magic sword. He held out his hand as if to reach for it, but at that moment he remembered the drawbridge had been entrusted to him alone.

"No!" he called out to the old man. "I will not leave my post!"

"Take it," cried the old man. "It is for you!" And he waved the sword high in the air.

Sir Roland became deeply afraid that if he listened to the old man's words any longer, or looked again at the shining sword, he would not be able to hold himself within the castle.

"I will not take it!" he cried.

At that moment an amazing thing happened. Across the moat the old man threw back his cloak, and as he did so, he began to grow bigger and bigger, until he stood the largest of all the giants in the forest. Sir Roland could scarcely believe his eyes. The giant shook his great fist across the moat, then turned and strode back to the forest.

T'was a good thing I heeded my lord's instructions, thought Sir Roland. *A good thing, indeed!*

Just then came a sound that made him spring forward in joy. Bugles pealed joyfully, triumphantly, as the weary knights made their way back to the castle. The battle was won!

Sir Roland greeted them all as they passed through the gate, and then followed them to take his place in the great hall of council.

Just as the lord of the castle was about to speak, one of the knights cried out, "The shield! The shield! Sir Roland's shield!"

Everyone turned and looked at the shield which Sir Roland carried on his left arm. There in its centre shone a bright golden star.

"Tell us, Sir Roland!" commanded the lord. "What happened at the castle today? Were you attacked? Have any giants come hither? Did you fight them alone?"

"No, my lord," replied Sir Roland. "Only one knight came here, and he left quietly when he found he could not enter."

And he went on to tell the lord all that had occurred at the gate.

No one spoke when he was finished. All eyes gazed at the golden star that shone brightly at the heart of the shield.

After a little silence the lord spoke. "The silver shield is not mistaken," he said. "Sir Roland has fought and won the hardest battle of the day."

Then the whole company arose as one and saluted Sir Roland, the youngest knight ever to have won the golden star.

Think about it

- Why was Sir Roland disappointed about the task he was given?
- Why do you suppose the lord of the castle chose Sir Roland to guard the gates?
- Who visited him while he guarded the castle? What were the reasons they gave for leaving his post?
- How did Sir Roland earn the golden star?
- What enemies did he fight and conquer? (His own anger and frustration; the desire to pursue his own glory rather than obey his orders; his natural tendency to retaliate to taunts and slander.)

Something to do

- Get the children to design and make a shield with a golden star in the centre. Present it each evening to the child that obeyed a difficult order. Let that child be the knight of honour for a day - the one who has won his star.

So said...

- "Through obedience learn to command." *Plato*
- "Obedience to authority saves many skins." *Sophocles*

Boom clip

When Katie was just two she loved to have play fights with Daddy. (She still does!) However this particular evening, she wriggled to escape her captor and ping! she dislocated her elbow. It was a long trip into Accident and Emergency. There, the doctor asked her to try and stay very still while he examined her arm. She obeyed, the whole time calling out, "Mummy! Daddy! Woey! [Her brother, Joe.] Ninny! [The dog.] Mummy! Daddy! Woey! Ninny!"

I couldn't help but cry as I watched her lie so still, calling out our names over and over. She won her golden star that night.

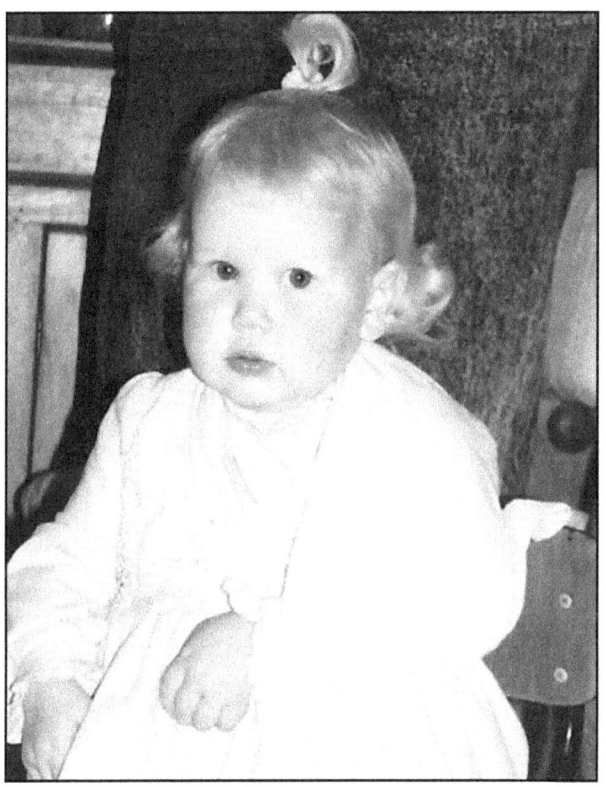

The patient

Words to live by

- "He who is slow to anger is better than the mighty, and he who rules his own spirit than he who takes a city." *Proverbs 16:32*

- "Hear O Israel, and be careful to obey so that it may go well with you, and so that you may enjoy long life." *Deuteronomy 6:3 NIV*

- "Moses said to them, 'Take to heart all the words I have solemnly declared to you this day, so that you may command your children to obey carefully all the words of this law. They are not just idle words for you - they are your life.'" *Deuteronomy 32:46, 47 NIV* (N.B. This verse says it all! We must take His words to heart, and obey carefully. Why? Because they are our very life!)

Obedience

Dig deeper

- Read *The Brave Buffalo Fighter* by John D Fitzgerald. We have just finished reading this as a family and enjoyed it very much. The Parker family leave their home in Missouri and join a wagon train west. It is an exciting story of courage and adventure based on the diary of ten-year old Susan Parker. The captain of the train demands absolute obedience from those travelling under his protection, and for good reason.

- Read the account of Joshua and the battle of Jericho in Joshua 6. Previously the people had promised their obedience to Joshua. "Whatever you have commanded us we will do, and wherever you send us we will go. Just as we fully obeyed Moses, so we will obey you." *Joshua 1:16, 17 NIV*

- Read *The Tale of Peter Rabbit* by Beatrix Potter with your younger children. He didn't like doing what he was told, but later wished he had.

- Joshua knew he needed their strict obedience if they were to take the city. Discuss what happens in Joshua chapter 7 with Achan's disobedience.

- Discuss and then sing together the hymn *Trust and Obey*. It has some great truths about obedience in its verses.

The Gift of Values

How to do a Bible study

This is a simple yet effective way to dig into God's Word and discover for yourself great treasures.

Essentials - pen, paper, cross reference Bible.
Extra non-essential helps - Concordance; study aids; Bible dictionary etc.

1. PRAY first and ask the Holy Spirit to come alongside and teach you *(John 14:26)*.

2. START WITH A VERSE THAT HAS ALREADY SPOKEN TO YOU during your own Bible readings (a rhema). It may be a verse that you felt the Lord was challenging you on. A rhema is an exciting thing to receive, but so often we take the one verse and leave it at that, where if we were to dig a little deeper, we would discover a treasure of gold. Think of the rhema as being the first tiny nugget of gold that indicates to a miner that he is digging in the right spot!

3. WRITE down your original verse and any associated thoughts, e.g. what the Lord spoke to you through it; why it blessed you; how it challenged you. Make it personal. Ask yourself questions: Who? What? When? How?

4. READ THE CONTEXT and the surrounding verses.

5. NOW LOOK UP ANY CROSS REFERENCES listed beside the original verse. Write them down with any thoughts.

6. LOOK UP CROSS REFERENCES OF THE ABOVE CROSS REFERENCES and any other verse that comes to mind. Write them all down. You'll soon find that the Lord is speaking to you along a certain line or theme - stick with it! Remember, it doesn't need to

be an exhaustive study on the topic. The most important thing is to hear what the Lord is saying to you.

7. ISOLATE several points within a verse if applicable. Then follow them through separately using the above method. e.g. *Acts 20:19:* "… serving the Lord with: 1… all humility; 2… in tears; 3… and in trials."

8. LOOK up the subject in a concordance if you like. I suggest you don't do this too early on or you'll quickly feel overwhelmed with hundreds of different verses to look up!

9. SUMMARIZE what the Lord is saying to you. Don't worry if the study is only short. I still have short studies I did when I was sixteen, and I always look them up if I'm doing a message on that topic. It never ceases to amaze me how they contain some real gems!

10. FILE your studies in alphabetical order. Over the years the Lord will lead you back to the same truths and subjects, but perhaps with a different emphasis. It will be encouraging to read your old studies and see how you've grown. When I went to Borneo as a missionary, I took with me all my precious studies, many of them done when I was a teenager, and yes, preached from them!

I pray God will really bless you as you "do your best to present yourself to God as one approved, a workman that doesn't need to be ashamed, and who correctly handles the word of truth." *2 Timothy 2:15 NIV*

Epilogue

It has been such a joy to write this book. I hope and pray that within its pages, you've found some good seed to plant in the hearts of your children. May it bring forth a hundred-fold! May the little acorns grow into great oaks.

I have already started writing *The Gift of Values - Volume Two*. In this book we will look at the following values:

> Generosity
> Self-control
> Encouragement
> Forgiveness
> Patience
> Compassion

If you would like to receive notification of when the book is published, please email Rose at *thegiftofvalues@rosieboom.com* and simply write 'The Gift of Values - Volume Two' in the message line. I will let you know as soon as it is released.

May your family be blessed!

Rosie

Acknowledgments

Thank you: To my parents, Evan and Leone Harris, for their life-long example of all the values in this book. Also for the use of character studies they prepared years ago for Christian schools.

To my twin sister, Penelope, for always cheering me on.

To my brother, Peter, for drawing the oaktree logo. For my birthday last year, Peter made me a beautiful silver medallion of the Tree of Life. We have since adopted it as our family crest, as Boom means 'tree' in Dutch. Our family verse is Jeremiah 17:7-8. I am thrilled to use the 'Boom' tree on this cover.

To Christopher Goj of Fontamentals for his wonderful help in editing and formatting.

To all the ladies at HEART who first asked me to write this book.

To Mum Boom for proof reading and praying.

To my friend Celia, who was such a support and encouragement to me in my early years of home schooling.

To my friend Altus, for letting me use his story about the blackballs.

To my wonderful children for preparing dinners, folding washing and giving me the time to write.

And to Chris - for loving me, believing in me, and encouraging me to write this book.

The Gift of Values

More from the Boom family album

A word from Peter, Rosie's brother who printed the first edition of this book and put the photos in:

This is one of the truly happy families that some say exist only in fond memory. My sister had a long wait to find the mythical 'Right Man', but find him she did! And their love and faithfulness have given a priceless gift to their children, which will be passed on through the generations. Is this "the Last Homely House" (to quote *The Hobbit)?* - I hope not! May Rosie's book inspire many to follow their shining example.

The photos that follow are like a few fallen leaves picked at random from under a great living oak, whose green leaves give shelter to many - birds, beasts and humans!

The 'silly expressions' photo

Milly and Eliza

Eliza reads to Jacob

Milly the Pirate with "Parrot" Raspberry
(Peter just had to give this a full page!)

The Family Album

Dad and Milly

Mum and Sam

Kate, Sam and Josiah

Pirates!

Chris and Rosie. Worth the wait ...

About the Author

Rosie lives with her husband, Chris, and their six children, Josiah, Kate, Eliza, Emily, Samuel and Jacob in Whangarei, New Zealand.

Rosie spent three years as a young child in Papua New Guinea, where her parents were missionaries. After graduating from her nursing training, she spent a year in Borneo as a missionary. It was here that Chris came to visit her and declare his love - the rest is history!

Rosie and Chris are singer/songwriters, and have had the joy of encouraging and challenging Christians in many different countries. They have released a number of CDs which are available on their website. Rosie has also published a children's book, *The Happy Prince*.

Rosie is a sought after speaker at women's conferences, missions and home-schooling conventions, and churches, where she loves to speak about her passions - missions, family, and Jesus.

For speaking engagements and bookings, contact Rosie at:

Boom Tree Publishing
Rosie Boom
549 Kara Rd, R.D. 9 Whangarei, New Zealand
Email: rosie@rosieboom.com
Rosie's Blog : www.rosieboom.com
Website: www.rosieboom.com

Other books by Rosie Boom

The Gift of Values - Volume 2

More creative ideas to teach your children the following values:
Self control   Compassion
Encouragement   Generosity
Patience   Forgiveness.

Printed hardcover, blue leather look with silver foil trim.

The Happy Prince

A re-telling of Oscar Wilde's story about a golden statue of a prince and the little swallow that alights at its feet one night on his way to Egypt. Includes a CD with the story told in a ten-minute song. Full page colour illustrations throughout.

The Barn Chronicles: Books 1–4

Where Lions Roar at Night

This book is the first in *The Barn Chronicles* series, and tells of the exciting, humorous adventures of the Boom family as they make their home in a 90-year-old barn. They are suitable for primary age readers, or to be read to children by parents.

Winner of the 2010 CALEB PRIZE for Best Children's Book

Where Arrows Fly

Where Arrows Fly is the sequel to *Where Lions Roar at Night* and is the second book in The Barn Chronicles series. Read about the continuing adventures of the Boom family and the everyday joys and challenges of the 'simple life'.

Winner of the 2011 CALEB PRIZE for Best Children's Book

Where the Crickets Sing

Where the Crickets Sing, the third book in *The Barn Chronicles* series, invites the reader to join the Boom family in another year of homesteading in rural New Zealand.

Finalist in the 2012 CALEB PRIZE for Best Children's Book
Winner 2013 Christian Small Publishers International Book of the Year Award Children's Category

Where the River Rises

As the Boom family begins a fourth year of living in their 93-year-old barn, a terrible drought has Northland in its grip. The time has finally come to leave the barn and begin a whole new adventure…

2013 CSP Book of the Year Award - Best Children's Book

Where the Jungle Calls

A long time before The Barn Chronicles, Rose lived in the big city. But one day her life changed forever...

Rose, Penny and Peter find themselves swept away into a great adventure, sailing the blue Pacific to a mission school deep in the jungles of Papua. There they become adventurers and explorers in their own wild kingdom. But there are hidden dangers lurking: snakes, scorpions, jerry-wars, malaria – and in the sea and rivers fearsome crocodiles…

Here in the jungles of New Guinea the readers of *The Barn Chronicles* will meet their favourite characters again in a different time, a different place. This is where their adventures first began.

www.ingramcontent.com/pod-product-compliance
Lightning Source LLC
Chambersburg PA
CBHW051129160426
43195CB00014B/2403